Education for life: a European Strategy

Education for life: a European Strategy

edited by **Dr. Kari Kairamo**

Butterworth Scientific Limited, UK, in collaboration with the Round Table of European Industrialists, Brussels

Butterworths
London   Boston   Singapore   Sydney   Toronto   Wellington

PART OF REED INTERNATIONAL P.L.C.

All rights reserved. No part of this publication may be reproduced or transmitted in any form or by any means, including photocopying and recording, without the written permission of the copyright holder, application for which should be addressed to the Publishers, or in accordance with the provisions of the Copyright Act 1956 (as amended), or under the terms of any licence permitting limited copying issued by the Copyright Licensing Agency, 7 Ridgmount Street, London WC1E 7AE, England. Such written permission must also be obtained before any part of this publication is stored in a retrieval system of any nature.

Any person who does any unauthorized act in relation to this publication may be liable to criminal prosecution and civil claims for damages.

This book is sold subject to the Standard Conditions of Sale of Net Books and may not be re-sold in the UK below the net price given by the Publishers in their current price list.

© Butterworth & Co (Publishers) Ltd, 1989

British Library Cataloguing in Publication Data

Education for life: a European strategy
  1. Western Europe. Vocational education
  I. Kairamo, Kari II. European
  370.11′3′094

ISBN 0-408-04514-0

Library of Congress Cataloging in Publication Data applied for

Printed in Great Britain by Anchor Press Ltd, Tiptree, Essex

CONTENTS

Acknowledgements   vii

Foreword   1

Part I: Exploration and Recommendations   5

1.	Revitalisation of Education	6
2.	Industry-Education Co-operation	8
3.	Technical and Professional Education	10
4.	Transferability and Compatibility	11
5.	Lifelong Learning and Adult Education	12
6.	A Framework for Action	14
7.	Education in the European Economic Space	16
8.	Industry's Opinions on Education	20
9.	Education and Training Activities of Some Companies	24

Part II: Educating Young People for the 21st Century   37

1.	Present Trends	39
2.	Major Issues	42
3.	The Thrust of Positive Action	47
4.	Industry Involvement	62

Part III: Higher Education: A European Imperative   77

1.	Scope and Objectives	78
2.	Comparisons between the European, North American and Japanese Systems	81
3.	Funding	84
4.	Engineering Education	87
5.	The Educational Perspective	90
6.	Company Needs	92
7.	Initiatives and Proposals for Action	95

Part IV: Vocational Education Across Europe   103

1.	Introduction	104
2.	Interaction with the Public VET System	107
3.	Strategic Capability and Flexible Responsiveness	107
4.	New Occupations and Technologies	108
5.	Skill Shortages	109
6.	Structures and Organisational Preferences	111
7.	Making Education and Training A Business	113
8.	Companies and the Public System	117

Part V: Management Development Practices   121

1.   European Management Education   122
2.   What the Survey Revealed   129
3.   Managerial Skills and Competences   140
4.   Comparison of Management Development Practices   145
5.   Company-wide Action Programmes   149
6.   The International Management Dimension   151
7.   Pinpointing Management Potential   153
8.   Coping with Demand Through Flexibility   158
9.   Supply of Teachers   160
10.   Open Learning Systems   162
11.   Development of A European Approach   164
12.   The European Management Model   166

Part VI: Lifelong Learning and Adult Education   169

1.   From Restructuring Industry to Restructuring Work   170
2.   The New Employee and New Values   171
3.   How is Industry Responding to the Changes?   171
4.   Adult Education - The Necessity Born of Restrucutring   173
5.   Obstacles to Progress in Adult Education   174
6.   Adult Education and Training Lack Models   175
7.   Still Largely a Company Responsibility   176
8.   Open Learning - A Key to Adult Education   177
9.   The Principles of Open Learning   177
10.   Organisation Based on Co-operation   179
11.   Work on Attitudes Needed on All Levels   180

Bibliography   181

Terminology   184

Main Contributors   189

ACKNOWLEDGEMENTS

This book, co-ordinated by Dr. Jan-Peter Paul, is the result of the joint effort of many individuals. The authors who made the primary contribution to each section are acknowledged in the chapter headings.

In 1987-1988, the Round Table conducted a survey of the education and training work being done by major European companies. The survey, on which this book is based, elicited opinions and conceptions concerning public education.

The 24 companies which participated are:

>Anova AG, Switzerland
>Asea AB, Sweden
>B.A.T., Industries, United Kingdom
>Daimler-Benz, West Germany
>Isvor-Fiat SpA, Italy
>Lafarge Coppée, France
>Nestlé S.A., Switzerland
>Nokia Corporation, Finland
>Norsk Hydro A.S., Norway
>Ing C Olivetti & C SpA, Italy
>Petrofina S.A., Belgium
>Philips International B.V., The Netherlands
>Pilkington plc, United Kingdom
>Pirelli SpA, Italy
>The Plessey Company plc, United Kingdom
>Robert Bosch GmbH, West Germany
>Siemens AG, West Germany
>Saint Gobain, France
>Societe Generale de Belgique, Belgium
>Telefónica de Espana S.A., Spain
>Thomson S.A., France
>Volkswagen AG, West Germany
>AB Volvo, Sweden
>Waterford Glass plc, Ireland

Photo Courtesy Nokia

FOREWORD

European industry, as well as the cost structure of its products, has become more knowledge-intensive. Therefore, a competitive advantage can be gained by raising employees' level of education and thus their competence. Skilled and well-educated people are vital for success. That was the principal reason why the **European Round Table of Industrialists** concluded that education is a strategic issue in European competitiveness.

The causes of the high unemployment rate in Europe, as documented in the Round Table publication "Making Europe Work" (1986), indicate that much of the increase in unemployment is caused by inappropriate or outdated education. At the same time, Europe lacks skilled labour in many professions and industries. Clearly, supply does not match demand in European education.

Europe allows and even encourages its young individuals to take the liberty of pursuing "interesting", not directly job-related studies, which in many cases have little prospect of practical application. At the same time, society is expected to provide full employment for everybody. This unbalanced situation is not eased by the fact that, in some countries, quotas for certain professions are maintained regardless of the law of supply and demand.

The question to be asked is: Does our educational system properly prepare people to live and work in Europe in the 21st century, and does it provide people with adequate new knowledge throughout their working life? The technical and industrial development of European industry clearly requires an accelerated revitalisation of education and its curricula. It also requires new opportunities and new models for updating and upgrading the skills and competence of Europe's working-age population.

The demography of the European workforce is changing and the working population is aging rapidly. The decline in student enrolments at professional schools and universities will be rather dramatic between 1990 and 2000. It is not unreasonable to suggest that the technological leadership of the West will be threatened in that event. A report issued in West

Germany warns that high-technology sectors of industry are already under pressure and raises the question of whether European scientists and engineers will be able to cope with international competition when they are, on average, 10 to 20 years older than their Asian competitors.

The likely consequence is that a lot of economic, political and technological assets will be transferred to Asian countries with rapidly growing populations. Multinationals are likely to gravitate toward these rapidly expanding markets. One of most important alternatives available to Europe is to discover ways of using the talents of older workers by means of refresher studies, retraining them and upgrading their competence. Learning should be a part of daily life and work. **Lifelong learning** should be adopted by modern Europe.

The countries within the European Economic Space are undergoing a rapid process of economic integration. However, arrangements for updating education and training have not been adequately envisioned, although the EC has begun this challenging work. Within EFTA and between the EC and EFTA, such efforts are practically non-existent. Education and training are still considered by many governments and decision makers as national matters and the new need to make education compatible as a means of integrating Europe is still being ignored.

To address these issues, the European Round Table of Industrialists established in 1987 a **Standing Working Group on Education** and asked it to identify the main problems related to European education and training from industry's point of view. The Group's goal was to draw up practical recommendations for education administrations, institutions and industry itself on how education in Europe could be improved and adjusted to keep pace with a constantly changing competitive environment.

The Working Group organised itself into four subcommittees, concentrating on the following aspects:

*   Basic Education
*   Higher Education
*   Vocational Education and Training
*   Management Training

Each subcommittee conducted a study and compiled a report, using the expertise within the ERT as well as that of external specialists. In addition, a special task force studied the question of **Lifelong Learning** and **Adult Education.**

The Working Group further carried out an industry survey to assess the opinions and expectations of ERT-related companies. A further goal was to determine how companies in Europe educate and train their own personnel. The findings of the subcommittees and the results of the industry survey have been compiled in this book.

Several companies, institutions and individuals contributed to the work. Members of the ERT Standing Working Group on Education, and all the subcommittee members and chairmen, have shown considerable interest and devoted much time to analysing the questions and preparing the report.

The dedication of those who participated has made it possible to complete the study regardless of the fact that the resources available to the ERT and outside experts were modest in view of the extremely wide and complicated range of questions to be dealt with.

As far as is known, this study - both the review work in which the four subcommittees studied various education levels in Europe and the industry survey - is the first investigation into education on a Europe-wide basis. It has provided both new information and stimulated new conclusions and proposals. The need for faster renewal of European education and for greater educational compatibility has become quite clear. Similarly, the necessity of creating a European concept of lifelong learning and the need for closer co-operation and partnership between all parties concerned with education and training has been identified.

                                                            Kari Kairamo

PART I
EXPLORATION AND RECOMMENDATIONS

1. REVITALISATION OF EDUCATION

Education in Europe is fundamentally sound and its academic quality is good. However, administrative practices are often too rigid to allow educational institutions at various levels to adapt to the changes made imperative by rapidly developing modern technology and the restructuring of industry and services. So far, these developments have not been taken adequately into consideration in creating new methods and curricula for European education.

Of particular concern are the quality, skills and competence of **teachers**. At present, no systematic policies exist for modernising the teacher training curricula, nor for retraining teachers. Teachers have few opportunities for career development and, most often, no experience in other professions. Additionally, the results of their work are difficult to measure and assess.

Young people today learn principally by visual experience. Since the need for individualised education is growing rapidly, at the same time as knowledge is fast becoming obsolete, new means of supplying appropriate basic education are obviously essential. These include **new tools and methods** such as computer-aided instruction, satellite programmes and other means.

Co-operation between the European media industry and educational institutions should be increased to develop more TV and video material covering a wide range of curricula and available in the major European languages for use within the European Economic Space.

Mathematics and the sciences form the basis for all technology. Thus they should play an adequate role in school curricula. Somehow these subjects are failing to attract young students. European school authorities could perform a valuable service by formulating a plan to revitalise the teaching and curricula of mathematics, physics, chemistry and natural sciences, and also determine minimum qualifications and requirements. It is in industry's interests to participate in and sponsor this work.

* Basic educational programmes are too rigid

* Basic education and working life are too far apart

* Education has not adapted to changes in technology and the restructuring of work

* A stronger concentration on mathematics, physics and new technology is needed

* New educational tools have had little acceptance

* TV and other media could co-operate more with educational institutions to provide teaching material

* Skills and competence of teachers need better updating

* Student exchange programmes are in need of development

2. INDUSTRY-EDUCATION CO-OPERATION

In contrast to the United States, co-operation between industry and educational institutions has traditionally been relatively weak in Europe. This is especially true of academic studies and research. Also, industry's influence on the curricula being developed has been weak, and this has adversely affected the real working skills of students entering employment after graduation.

Several methods can be employed to improve co-operation:

* Industry support for major EC and other European educational programmes, such as COMETT and Euro-PACE, deserve encouragement in order to strengthen and widen the scope of adult education in industry.

* Development of partnerships between universities/colleges and industry within post- and under-graduate programmes and in vocational training courses is necessary. Several models reflecting this concept emerged from the survey. However, most of these were local or regional in character. Programmes like NORIT, U-LINK and TARGET (a COMETT programme successfully implemented in the U.K.) provide good starting points for further expansion and development on a multilateral basis. Some companies have initiated models for industry/university co-operation. The development and enhancement of these models on a wider basis, not only at the level of higher education but also within vocational education and training, could be encouraged.

* To improve the continuous interaction between industry and education, it is recommended that the administrative bodies of schools and universities admit greater representation on the part of companies, which could also participate in the development of the curricula and other teaching tools.

In order to make university and college education more related to the world of work, it is desirable for teachers and professors to have working experience in industry. Opportunities to organise various apprenticeship programmes for teachers warrant study. Industry's contribution here could be to encourage its own personnel to act as part-time teachers. More - also international - apprenticeships and schemes combining school and work-based learning are recommendable to provide young people with the opportunity to have a basic facility for a vocation. Apprenticeship in industry could be an obligatory part of all secondary education. Educational advisors to the British government have recommended that work experience be given to all pupils before they leave school.

To enhance co-operation between companies in the field of education and training and broaden models for company-university co-operation, a forum of education and training managers of the European industry could be considered. The education and training managers of certain companies that participated in the survey had, in 1987, organised a meeting to discuss their educational and training activities and experiences.

---

* Co-operation between industry and educational institutions in Europe lags behind the USA and Japan
* Industry's influence on curricula and qualifications is too weak
* Local and regional industry-university co-operation programmes could be expanded
* More industry involvement in EC and other European educational programmes is desirable
* More industry representation on the administrative bodies of schools and universities is recommended
* Apprenticeships for teachers in industry
* Encouraging company employers to act as part-time teachers
* More - also international - apprenticeship schemes at all levels of education

---

3. TECHNICAL AND PROFESSIONAL EDUCATION

There is a positive correlation between technical competence and business success. The importance of technology is not, however, reflected in the educational priorities of Europe:

* there are only 39 graduates in technology per 100,000 inhabitants in Europe, while the figures for the US and Japan are 77 and 76, respectively
* there is a chronic shortage of engineers in many new areas of technology
* companies' training activities are concentrated on management and general issues and based on short-term ad hoc courses. Effective, long-term, targeted studies in major fields of modern technology for personnel and working adults are still very rare in Europe
* at the level of higher education, technical studies do not attract students as much as, for example, the humanities.

Technology and technical competence can give companies a competitive edge. All new ways and means should be used to improve technical education all over Europe and to use more effectively the European teaching resources in the field of technology.

---

* The importance of technology is not properly reflected in the educational priorities of Europe
* Constant shortages of engineers in many new technologies
* Technical studies are not attractive enough to young students
* New needs for continuous education, basic and theoretical competence are not receiving enough attention. Training will not be effective if basic education is weak
* Training provided by most companies is concentrated on general issues and management based on short-term ad hoc courses. Technical competence demands longer term education
* A European framework for continuously upgrading education in the important fields of technology could be developed to integrate knowledge and teaching resources

4. TRANSFERABILITY AND COMPATIBILITY

European education is founded on national premises and on widely diverging basic ideologies. Faced with European economic integration and the free movement of labour, national thinking needs to be replaced by a unified European concept.

Industry gives full support to the work of the EC in its efforts to seek transferability and compatibility and develop European education, as well as to promote the use of modern technology in enhancing the compatibility of education. The concept of European educational programmes could be applied at various educational levels, and throughout the European Economic Space.

A special issue in European culture is multilingualism. It is therefore of the utmost importance that a European can converse in the major languages of Europe. Tailoring school curricula to contain a **minimum of three languages** in every European country represents the real values of Europe's civilisation and recognition of a strength that ought to be fully utilised.

---

* European education is founded on national premises and divergent national ideologies
* Transferable and compatible minimum qualifications and degrees for professional
* Compatibility of core curricula in Europe
* Three European languages in each basic school curriculum

---

5. LIFELONG LEARNING AND ADULT EDUCATION

The concept of work is continuously changing. An individual not only has several jobs in a lifetime, but may also have several careers. Therefore, everybody needs a continuous updating and upgrading of skills and competence throughout working life.

Europe does not have enough effective and motivational models and practices for adult education, especially for adults who would study while working. Education at all levels is for young, full-time students. It is almost impossible for people in employment to study while working. The linkage with academic and professional studies is too tenuous. Basic programmes organised by educational institutions are sometimes too theoretical and do not inspire the sacrifices that re-education demands.

It is also clear that people cannot be trained if they do not have sufficient new basic education.

In view of the imminent shortage of labour in Europe, it is even more important to have all possible age groups in continuous employment. Learning anew should thus take place alongside work. Lifelong learning should become an attitude and a practice. Present attitudes to education will have to change.

In order to facilitate the concept of **Lifelong Learning**, industry and educational institutions could work in close co-operation, developing tailor-made curricula for the re-education and further education of adult employees while they remain in their jobs. After qualification, such studies not only could, but should result in the award of a degree. Where appropriate, they would be complemented by joint research projects to familiarise employees with scientific thinking and methods.

Institutions like the **Open University** should spread to European countries, with arrangements between administrations to co-ordinate the development of curricula, educational software and programme exchanges between countries, universities and industries. The possibility of establishing a European Open University could be studied.

The concept of **Open learning** could be enhanced by establishing **a European Educational TV Network.**

Professional studies could be accepted as part of the credit in the educational system. The concept of professional competence acquired outside the academic environment could also be brought into the credit structure of universities and other institutions of higher education.

---

* Lifelong learning should become the guiding principle

* Politicians, opinion leaders, trade unions and industry alike should do their utmost to improve adult education

* Educational institutes should change to accommodate the new demands of adult students

* Companies should generate an atmosphere in which competence and education are esteemed and supported. Education has to be viewed as an investment in line with corporate strategy

* Competence and education are an individual's assets. It is up to individuals themselves to update and upgrade this capital in order to preserve their personal competitiveness and develop to meet the new demands of the working environment. Opportunities for studies alongside work could be provided.

* Open learning is one of the new models incorporating schools, teachers, satellite programmes, and other facilities in providing and distributing education

* Open University-type activities both nationally and within a European context are needed

* European educational TV network could be created

---

6. A FRAMEWORK FOR ACTION

European education could be given a fresh start by adopting models similar to those already applied in R&D. One such might be a programme for the advancement and co-ordination of research into the development of education in various European countries; a tentative name for this model might be EURED (or "European Unified Research into Educational Development"). EURED could become a framework for the advancement of education in Europe. It would be based on co-operation between

* legislative and regulatory bodies, such as national and European education authorities

* providers of education, such as universities, schools and institutes

* users of education, such as industry and the service sector

Some parts of the framework to be considered are:

EURED STANDARDS, as a co-operative project between national and European authorities, together with selected educational institutions, for facilitating the transferability of degrees

EURED TEACHER TRAINING, as a co-operative programme for improving and updating teacher training at all levels. The principal theme is the education of the existing workforce, with emphasis on:

* updating the knowledge and skills of teachers

* imparting/renewing the skills and knowledge for teaching contemporary subjects like information technology, computer science and telecommunication.

EURED SCIENTIFIC, as a host of scientifically oriented postgraduate programmes catering for the educational needs of European research programmes, such as EUREKA, BRITE, ESPRIT and RACE, with the purpose of disseminating the knowledge created by these projects throughout Europe

EURED OPEN STUDIES, as a co-operative project on the part of national authorities and users of education, aimed at enhancing the development and use of different modes of open education

EURED LIFELONG LEARNING, as a joint development programme organised by selected institutions and users of education to develop and promote the concept of lifelong learning

7. EDUCATION IN THE EUROPEAN ECONOMIC SPACE

Education and training within Europe are characterised by two major features - their historical roots and the present rapidity of change. Current educational and training systems have evolved over many centuries. The origin is found in the Middle Ages when the church catered for the educational needs of society. After the French Revolution (1789-1799) general school systems based on compulsory education were introduced on a national level in order to strengthen nationhood and citizenship. The pressures and requirements of the industrial revolution had effects on curricula, especially where technical subjects related to vocational education were concerned. A strong national educational system was the basis of schooling. Each nation emphasized different aspects in education, which reflected a strong cultural identity. The emphasis was on imprinting the unique cultural characteristics of each nation. National differences were emphasised and highlighted, not a mutual heritage. This led to different curricula and school structures for each nation state. Thus terms like school, college and other educational institutions are not directly comparable in different European countries.

The situation today is not related to the requirements of nationhood or basic industrial educational needs. In a unifying Europe with a free labour market and transferability and compatibility of skills the requirements on the educational systems are different. Today similarities are sought, not differences. The concept of strong nationalism has been taken over by Europeanism. Diversity and separate identity should be overcome and exchanged for educational systems which are mutually strengthening and supportive.

Education accounts on average for 5% of GDP in OECD countries. With few exceptions, public investment in education varies between 4 and 7% of GDP. The EFTA countries spent an average of 6.2% of GDP on education in 1980. The EC countries spent an average of 5.4% in the same year. The United States invested 5.6% and Japan slightly less, 5.5%.

Table 1. Public expenditure on education as % of GDP in current prices

	1970	1980	1981	1982	1983	1985
Austria	4.6	5.5	5.7	5.9	5.9	5.2
Denmark	6.7	6.6	-	-	-	6.5
Finland	5.9	5.4	5.5	5.5	-	5.4
France	-	5.1	5.2	-	-	4.8
Greece	2.1	2.2(2)	-	-	-	3.7
Ireland	5.0	6.3	6.7	6.2	-	4.4
Italy	4.6(1)	5.0	5.5	5.5	-	5.1
Japan	3.1	5.5	5.5	5.4	-	4.6
Luxembourg	4.6	7.4	7.6	8.3	-	6.4
Netherlands	6.8	7.6	7.4	7.3	-	5.3
Norway	6.0	5.9	6.2	6.3	6.3	5.0
Portugal	-	4.1	4.4	4.2	-	3.5
Sweden	7.2	9.0	8.4	8.2	7.6	5.8
Switzerland	4.1	5.2	5.1	5.2	-	-
United Kingdom	5.3	5.5	5.4	5.4	5.3	4.4
United States	6.4	5.6	-	-	-	5.8
West Germany	3.7	4.7	4.7	4.6	4.4	4.4

(1) 1971
(2) 1979
Source: OECD 1987, 83, and national authorities

Figures for Belgium are not available for 1970-1983. In 1984 and 1985 Belgium's public expenditure as a percentage of GDP in current prices was 5.9.

This means that Europe invests the same or more in education than the United States or Japan. One of the main problems in Europe's case is the selectivity and allocation of this investment. The recommendations presented earlier in this paper highlight the ways in which the Round Table would like to have some of these investments reallocated.

Expenditure by companies on training is subject to variation. In 1984, United States employers spent $30 billion on the formal training of 15 million employees and $180 billion on informal in-company training. In contrast, the United Kingdom compares very unfavourably with its main competitors in terms of investment in training by industry. For example, expenditure on training per employee is £1,500 in the United States, while it is only £200 in the United Kingdom. In West Germany, it is estimated that more than one million adult employees receive continuing education each year, half of which is provided by companies. In Japan, about 80 per cent of all firms implement some form of training and one third of all workers participate in formal courses. In France, company expenditure within the framework of the 1972 Training Act amounted to 14.7 billion FF in 1982, and involved 113.5 million hours of training (OECD 1988,7).

The companies surveyed by the Round Table stated that they invest on average about 2% of their wage totals in education, the highest figure being 6.3% (Siemens, Germany, 1987). Most Round Table companies are increasing their investments in education. French companies spend more than the minimum legal requirements of 1.1% of wages on education. The figures above are not directly comparable because of the content of what is included in various companies' figures. Some companies, for example in West Germany, have included the cost of apprenticeship. In other cases accommodation and travel costs at courses are included and sometimes they are not. There are also various national discrepancies. In France, where there is a minimum legal required for education, high figures may be sought. In other cases this may be irrelevant. To a significant extent various national accounting practice influence the funds spent on education. No unified practices on a European level can be identified.

The training and education responsibility assumed by industry has increased in recent years. In Sweden, for example, firms are giving basic education on company time to an increasing extent; 0.27% of wages go to supporting public adult training, not necessarily company specific. In 1985 the Swedish government took 10% of company profits (in the form of a special tax) for "personnel renewal fund", i.e. a fund to be used within 5 years for the education of its personnel, with the remainder forfeited to the State after that.

Most young people go to school until the age of 16-17, after which enrolment figures fall rapidly. At 17 more than 70% still attend some form of school, but at 18 the figure falls to approximately 50%, and at 19 it is only 36% (OECD, 1987, 72).

International statistics in education are not directly comparable. For example, in some European countries, many young people continue upper-secondary level education one or more years after finishing school at 18.

The percentage of 17 year olds attending educational institutions is highest in West Germany, Sweden and Japan, followed by the U.S. and some small European countries like Holland, Belgium and Switzerland. Japan and the U.S. are the only countries besides Canada where a majority of students obtain the credentials necessary for entering a university.

In West Germany, Austria and Switzerland, the majority of upper-secondary students are apprentices who undergo part-time, general education in schools for 1 or 2 days a week. In these countries the system is selective and only a small proportion of students have an opportunity to study at university level. In the rest of Europe, upper-secondary education is usually split between general and vocational streams. In the United Kingdom, for example, apprenticeships do exist and are regarded as of increasing importance. Vocational training is now generally seen as a very important part of the educational and training scene there. Those who follow on from general secondary education normally continue with high school and often move on to academic studies.

The OECD (1987) notes that a comparison of the vocational training systems in Europe, Japan and the United States reveals two fundamental differences. First, much of the vocational training in Europe is given at the secondary level, while in Japan and the United States most of it belongs to the post-secondary sphere and tends to start at somewhat higher ages. Secondly, training in Europe - especially in the German-speaking region - is more standardised and integrated into the regular education system.

8. INDUSTRY'S OPINIONS ON EDUCATION

In the survey conducted by the Round Table the interview partners were asked to comment on education by educational level. In the table below a synopsis of some characteristic concerns are given by geographical region.

Concerning **basic education**, i.e. education in the primary and secondary level, the main difficulties could be found in the general need to raise the level. In other words educational standards were found to be too low to match the competence requirements of industry. The respondents highlighted the need to develop communication skills and the ability to work in teams, with the emphasis on problem-solving capabilities. Another shortcoming identified was a poor understanding of the economic environment and the nature of business and profit making.

The respondents looked for a general change in teachers' attitudes to the realities of economic life. Without an understanding of what goes on in the real world a mismatch between what is produced by schools and expected by industry will continue.

One of the reasons for deficiencies in education and teaching was found in the present attitudes of primary and secondary school teachers. They are either not properly motivated, or lack the capability to promote the emergence of more flexible and adaptable forms of basic education, allowing for several careers in the future.

Comments by education and training managers of major European companies differed little from one region to another. On the other hand, regional differences were identified in the case of **vocational education and training (VET)**.

Table 2. **OPINIONS CONCERNING COMPANIES' PROBLEMS, SURVEYED WITH RESPECT TO EDUCATION ON VARIOUS LEVELS**

Level of Education	German	Latin	English	Scandinavian
Basic, general education (primary and secondary education)	The general level of competence should be improved. On the whole, everything could be better. Need for: Core curriculum Problem areas: Teachers' attitudes Lack of understanding of the economic environment	The capability to learn should be improved as well as general behaviour and languages. Need for: Teamwork Problem areas: Languages Teachers' attitudes Lack of understanding the economic environment	General level of competence should be improved, skills and the ability to solve problems. The capability to learn should also be improved. Need for: Core curriculum Communication skills Problem-solving skills Problem areas: Discipline Effectiveness Teachers' attitudes Lack of understanding the economic environment	General level of competence should be improved, as well as communication skills. Need for: Communication skills Language skills Problem areas: Attitudes Languages Reading/writing Teachers' attitudes
Teachers' attitudes (Basic education)	Indifferent and don't understand	Indifferent, but beginning to understand industry needs	Don't understand industry needs	Don't understand industry needs and in general are indifferent
Industrial retraining	The companies are satisfied with the public VET system Need for: Languages Ability to work in teams Mathematics Problem-solving Problem areas: Contacts between VET institutions and industry Transferability Major areas of retraining: EDP, informatiques, data processing, management and commercial skills, languages, environmental subjects	The VET given in public institutions doesn't match industry needs, i.e. in technical areas, economic thinking and crafts Need for: Ability to learn Languages Problem areas: The need for formalised contacts Transferability Major areas of retraining: Languages, math, computers, management skills, electronics	The standards given by public institutions don't match industry needs as to languages and crafts Need for: Learning skills Problem-solving skills Problem areas: VET standards Transferability Major areas of retraining: Languages, management, marketing, data processing	In general satisfied. Criticism concerning narrow training base, mechanics Need for: Communication skills Problem areas: The lack of new VET Transferability Major areas of retraining: Electronics, management, security, mechanics
Higher education	The level of education is mainly good Need for: engineers, biologists, accountants, computer scientists Major areas of retraining: Technical and applied studies, business, languages, informatiques	The level of education in general is good or very good Need for: Auditors, marketing people, electronics specialists Major areas of retraining: Management, engineering, marketing, electronics, material studies	The level of education in general is good Need for: Engineers in informatiques, technology and electronics Major areas of retraining: Management, engineering, marketing, electronics, material studies	The level of education is good Need for: Financial people, computer specialists and informatiques Problem areas: Flexibility, less rigidness Major areas of retraining: Electronics, material studies, finance, management
Main issues regarding education	Communication abilities Holistic thinking Business initiative Management Broad education Problem-solving	Flexibility Management Communication skills	Communication skills Business administration Strategic thinking	Management Business administration Internationalisation Culture

Respondents in the German-speaking region were quite satisfied with the public VET system. This satisfaction was not, however, without qualification. There seemed to be additional needs for language training and mathematics. Some attitude changes were also sought in relation to problem-solving and the ability to work in a team. In order to remedy these deficiencies still closer contacts were sought between VET institutions and industry.

In the Latin region the VET institutions and industry seem to be moving apart, as they do not follow industry's needs, for example in some technical areas, crafts and languages. The educational methods also seemed lacking as the students had an insufficient ability to learn. Suggestions to solve these problems pointed to closer formalized contacts between VET institutions and industry.

Similar difficulties were perceived in the English-speaking region, where the standards of public institutions are not considered to match industry needs. There is a need for problem-solving and learning skills, in addition to which VET standards are lacking in transferability.

In the Scandinavian region industry seemed to be quite satisfied with education and training related to VET. Some criticism was expressed concerning too little training time and emphasis on mechanical engineering. There appeared to be a general need for the enhancement of communication skills.

In all regions the question of international transferability and comparibility was highlighted as being the major singular problem area. There was a clear demand for transferable VET degrees throughout Western Europe. Several areas of retraining needs were specified, knowledge of languages being the major one. Other subjects in which retraining was found to be necessary included information technology, electronics, mechanics, mathematics, management and commercial skills. Environmental subjects were also mentioned as one area of retraining deserving special attention.

Higher education (i.e. college and university) is considered part of public education. The number of people with higher education or post-graduate degrees employed by the companies surveyed represented an average of 10% of their total workforces. The highest proportion of employees with higher education degrees is in the defence industry, followed by the oil, electronics and automotive industries. The academics were also often young and had only recently entered working life. No significant national differences could be identified.

An education in an area of technology is the most highly valued basis for employment in industry. The companies surveyed complained of difficulty in recruiting engineers in sufficient numbers, with demand remaining high. The main demand was in the fields of electronics, computer science, logistics, chemistry and information technology.

The demand for graduates in most fields is expected to continue throughout the 1990s, and even to increase in some countries. Most companies pointed out that there will be a continuous marginal increase in the number of graduates in their company. This is especially true for the electronics, telecommunications, automotive and defence industries.

In general, the companies were satisfied with the level of knowledge possessed by newly hired graduates. Most assessed the level of basic education as good or very good. The level of applied knowledge was considered either satisfactory or good. The best marks were awarded by German, Latin and Scandinavian companies. The electronics and telecommunications sectors were most satisfied.

In many instances graduates' education was complemented within companies, notably those in the electronics, telecommunications and automotive industries. Only seldom was education complemented outside the company.

Besides dealing with concrete subjects, retraining is also expected to engender a new attitude. Graduates from universities and other institutions of higher education should be equipped with the ability to think holistically and have the capability to communicate and take initiative. They should be in general aware of what takes place around them; thus their educational background should be broad, including a sense of culture.

9. EDUCATION AND TRAINING ACTIVITIES OF SOME COMPANIES

Most of the Round Table companies have a system of training and education to enhance in-house skill formation and thus competence.

All these systems and programmes have been adapted to specific demands and the local environment. Some companies with extensive and well-managed and organised training and education activities are described here.

In West Germany, Daimler-Benz AG and Siemens AG are presented, in Switzerland Holderbank and Nestlé, in the United Kingdom Pilkington, and in Scandinavia Nokia and Volvo. All these companies represent the latest developments in education and training and are breaking ground in the application and introduction of new models.

The German companies have adapted their models to the strong tradition of a publicly funded apprenticeship system. The Swiss companies are involving managers on a wide scale as teachers, and Pilkington is finding new ways to enhance the training of young school leavers. This company is also extensively involved on the British national scene in the promotion of new ideas in most fields related to VET.

The Nordic companies are in the process of developing close co-operation with public educational institutions on all levels. Volvo, for example, is engaged in giving basic, primary education to some of its employees. Nokia is co-operating with the national educational system to give its employees the possibility to acquire various levels of degrees while at work.

West Germany

Daimler-Benz AG is one of the major industrial concerns in West Germany and a significant manufacturer of automobiles. Its sales in 1987 amounted to 67 billion DM. The company employs more than 320,000 people globally.

Daimler-Benz gives 2 million hours of training, excluding management training, to its employees. In 1987 more than 82,000 of them took part in some form of training. The main emphasis was on high technology fields, with special attention to young people. The total amount spent on education and training amounted to 354 million DM, or 5.8% of personnel costs in 1987.

The company has three main forms of structured education and training: (1) continued education, (2) management education and training, and (3) non-structured continued education programmes. The latter category includes subjects like computer science, technology, languages, how to speak and learn, and introductory courses are included.

Management education and training is divided into three main parts: (1) general continued education, (2) continued education related to Daimler-Benz, and (3) international seminars and courses. General continued education includes subjects like the Daimler-Benz introductory seminar, strategic planning and decision-making, problem-solving, personal work planning, how to argue, discuss and convince. The Daimler-Benz-related continued education includes company policy, the company and society, and how to lead and develop business units. The international seminars and courses emphasise company policy and strategic planning.

The major role of unstructured programmes is unique for Daimler-Benz. In addition to job-related subjects in technology and business, there are not only language studies and leisure-related subjects, but also subjects like how to communicate at the workplace and within the family. Education is directly placed under a board member.

Funding is both centralised and decentralised. All education is co-ordinated centrally. The central organisation has its own budget but each business unit is required to invest a certain amount annually in training and education.

Siemens AG, with sales in 1986 exceeding 47 billion DM and more than 360,000 employees, is one of the largest and most significant companies in West Germany.

The use of new technologies in manufacturing and in the office has had an effect on the structure of the work and on the qualifications required of employees. The number of engineering assignments continues to rise, while the proportion of manufacturing jobs, particularly for unskilled workers, is becoming smaller. There is every indication that shifts in the workforce structure will continue. Siemens AG employs about 192,000 people in West Germany. 40,300 of them (21%) are graduates of universities and Fachhochschulen.

Training and continuing education is a primary concern of Siemens personnel policy. Expenditure for this purpose, like capital investments and R&D expenses, has been raised over the past few years. In 1987 it totalled approximately 840 million DM, which represents 6.3% of total wages and salaries.

The amount spent by Siemens AG on vocational training in 1987 came to 310 million DM. The expense related to continued education amounted to 530 million DM.

The training and development programmes include vocational training and retraining schemes for employees, internships, specialised and general continuing education sessions, and advanced training courses for teaching staff and management personnel. Siemens itself trains a major portion of its skilled workers, commercial staff, and technical assistants. At present there are some 15,000 trainees on the work force, about 400 of them young people from abroad.

Siemens offers training in 60 different manufacturing, commercial, and technical occupations. The emphasis is on training in manufacturing skills, in accordance with the German Dual System. About two-thirds of the 10,940 manufacturing apprentices are being prepared for a career in electrical engineering or electronics, and about one-third are learning a metal-working trade. The ratio of trainees in the total skilled workforce (45,300) is 24%. Manufacturing training at Siemens involves instruction in more than 50 industrial occupations and at some 70 trainee workshops and training centres.

Some 1,000 instructors trained in pedagogical methods are working in this sector. An even greater number of part-time training staff give young people initial guidance during their formal traineeships in workshops, offices, and on installation or construction sites.

Among the trainees are 2,000 young women; 600 of them are being prepared for jobs in manufacturing, 500 for technical occupations, and 900 for commercial positions.

On completion of their intermediate examinations, gifted university students, particularly those studying technical or scientific subjects, may join the "Siemens Student Circle for Engineers", giving them access to seminars, scholarships, internships, and specialist literature. For students of economics and business administration who have performed well in their intermediate examinations, the Siemens "Corporate Curriculum Programme" provides systematic courses of preparatory and complementary study.

The Siemens comprehensive continuing education scheme is open to all employees. The special courses and seminars offered deal with product- and function-oriented as well as interdisciplinary subjects. In addition, a large number of management development courses are held. These in-house programmes are complemented by continuing education on the job and participation in events, courses and programmes arranged by external institutions, such as technical academies, universities, engineering societies and others.

Each year, about 180,000 employees participate in a total of about 15,000 continuing education sessions and events in West Germany. This is equivalent to approximately 5 million course attendance hours per year. Two-thirds of the continuing education programmes deal with new in-house products and processes. Approximately 25% of the continuing education programmes are revised every year on the basis of new developments and information.

Systematic continuing education seminars and courses are held at product-oriented schools. Basic interdisciplinary subjects of a technical and business nature, foreign languages, organisation and methods, and management development are dealt with at training centre sessions. The regional offices and plants are responsible for seminars relevant to special regions. There are special continuing education programmes for executive personnel and teaching staff. If required, in-house programmes are developed and run in close co-operation with specialised institutes, universities and Fachhochschulen.

At the training centres, regional offices, and plants, Siemens provides an increasing number of self-tutoring stations, which employees can use to continue their education individually. In addition, a number of correspondence courses, consisting of both lessons and training phases, are offered. This is especially important for locations without a training centre.

Continuing education courses are organised with a staff of 700 teaching professionals and 3,000 part-time instructors. One advantage of having part-time instructors who are still active in industry, particularly if they are senior executives, is that new methods and developments can be immediately put into practice.

Special emphasis is placed on "training the trainers". Instructors in the manufacturing and technical areas, for example, participate in a four-week programme of seminars culminating in a teaching aptitude examination. Numerous advanced seminars are also offered to enhance and expand the teaching proficiency and knowledge of the training staff.

Switzerland

Nestlé with sales in 1987 exceeding 35 billion CHF and 163,000 employees is an industrial group consisting of 200 operating units of different sizes that share a common culture. This structure is compatible with the diversified nature of their activities and enables the individual companies to maintain their intimacy and distinctive characteristics as the group grows larger.

The operating companies enjoy a great deal of independence within the guidelines of long-term policies established for the Group and adapted to local conditions. It operates some 360 factories on five continents, half of these factories have fewer than 200 employees. Nestlé as a multinational group is mainly concerned with food and body care products, which it produces in over fifty countries.

Nestlé is organised in a highly decentralised way and management emphasises products and people more than the strict application of abstract systems. An important factor in human development is training, which is mainly decentralised. Operating units are required to offer training opportunities to their managers, employees and workers. However, the company places special emphasis on the development of managers and specialists and offers at its International Training Centre in Switzerland a large variety of seminars and workshops. Nestlé has worldwide about 10,000 managers and highly specialised staff to be trained, the philosophy being to "train and motivate Nestlé employees worldwide to make positive contributions to the attainment of the Group's objectives and to improve its long-term competitive position". On the other hand, the company acknowledges that each individual is responsible for his or her personal development, which cannot be substituted for by the company. An important aspect is the on-the-job training, which cannot be replaced by formal training, but the latter is an appreciated complement. The three main objectives with training are (1) maintain and improve knowledge and work skills, (2) accelerate the development of those with potential for advancement, and (3) assist those who move to new assignments which require training.

Apart from these basic objectives, training activities should help to foster corporate culture and a sense of Group identity, for which the Training Centre is an ideal place, also considering that 75% of the teaching is done by Nestlé managers, specialists and trainers. Another important aspect is the exchange of experience, with participants from all over the world.

A special group is prepared for an international career. An initial on-the-job training mixed with class-room seminars is offered during a period of 1½-2½ years. For this group it is especially essential to look after the company's interests as though they were one's own, through (1) mobility or the willingness and ability to move both physically, i.e. from one geographical area to another, and socially, (2) adaptability both in geographical and intellectual terms, and (3) linguistic skill. The minimum requirement is for two languages, the preference being for English, French and Spanish.

Attitudes that are sought include a critical and positive mind, a certain humility to learn new basic skills, acceptance of the hierarchic system and the Nestlé system for appraisals and to be action-oriented and get things done.

Holderbank, the Swiss holding company with sales of 3.4 billion CHF and more than 19,000 employees in 21 countries, through the Ernst Schmidheiny Foundation, has directed "Holderbank" Management and Consulting Ltd. to develop a one week study course in economics for students in high-level teachers' training colleges and grammar schools.

The Economic Week is a varied teaching programme which gives the participants basic knowledge of business and economics. The instructors, mainly executives from a large number of Swiss enterprises, are all practitioners and teaching always features practical examples taken from the business life of the teaching staff.

United Kingdom

Pilkington plc is one of the world's leading manufacturers of glass and glass-related products. It is also a world leader in vision care products, electro-optical systems, and glass and mineral wool. It employs nearly 58,000 people.

The company is divided into several operating divisions and functions. Included in Group Personnel Services is the Group Training and Development Department which has the following roles:

- to advise the Board on human resource development (H.R.D.) strategies, methods and technologies;
- to keep abreast of advances in H.R.D.;
- to provide an internal consultancy on H.R.D. education and training to companies in the group;
- to manage the central training units providing a range of training events for operating units.

It is estimated that in Europe the Group spends about £5M annually on training and education. This figure excludes the salaries and wages of trainees during training.

Every division and operating unit is responsible for education, training and development of its human resources. The line management is responsible for effecting this policy, with the Personnel Director of each division having the overview. Divisions are free to use whatever resources are available locally, in-company or external, in order to implement their education and training policies. They call on the Group Training and Development Department to help them as and when required.

Sixteen year old school leavers are recruited into the three training schemes, initially for a two year programme run as part of the national Youth Training Scheme. These include engineering, production and administration.

In addition to the 16 year old intake in the administration area, a small number of trainees with a higher level of qualifications are taken on at

18. These trainees undergo an accelerated training programme, achieving in 1 year what the 16 year olds cover in 2 years.

Programmes of adult training are provided to meet business needs and/or individual qualification requirements. A series of courses is also run for supervisors at all stages of development, in addition to a range of demand-based courses in marketing and selling.

Newly recruited graduates attend a series of courses aimed at integrating them quickly into the company. All new graduates are expected, during their first two years, to study part-time for qualifications including: Diploma in Management Studies, Institute of Marketing, Institute of Purchasing and Buying, and Institute of Personnel. In addition, they would attend courses in their specialist subjects at universities and other training organisations.

All managers should expect to attend an executive development course at the start of their managerial careers. This sets the scene and shares with them the Pilkington culture and policies. Those managers with potential are nominated in succession plans, and individual career plans are fed into annual training plans.

After the initial management development course, managers will proceed to the next internal programme, which concentrates on business development, the individuals' development following that of the business.

All managers who are appointed directors of companies attend a programme at the Institute of Directors dealing with their legal responsibilities. Directors who have been in their post for some time, may attend an in-house Director Development Programme.

Schools, colleges and universities are used where their products are relevant to Pilkington's business needs. In the U.K. there are many institutions which are the guardians of professional standards, conduct and ethics. These have the right to ensure that as many employees as possible have learned and understand the theory and have the practical skills they need. Competence implies possession of both.

The Nordic Countries

Nokia stresses that competitiveness depends on the competence of its employees. The extremely rapid development in all fields of technology makes it necessary continuously to update knowledge and skills as well as to acquire new expertise. This demands constant motivation. Nokia offers its employees the opportunity to develop and educate themselves while working and obtain a generally accepted degree. Its training activities are based on co-operation with universities and other educational institutes, which offer a formal training setting, professional teachers and performance evaluation.

The target is to upgrade the expertise of half of its employees by one education level within the next ten years.

To achieve this goal, Nokia has implemented a number of technology training programmes: Ph.D., M.Sc. Eng., B.Sc. Eng., and continuous training and vocational education for workers.

Each Nokia employee applies for the training programme needed. Participants are selected in relation to the themes with which they are currently working or will be in the near future. The university or institute approves the students to be enroled and sets the level that studies have to meet. The university is responsible for the standard of instruction, and evaluates study performances.

The post-graduate courses are integrated with Nokia's internal research projects and the training needs are determined by the various divisions of the Nokia Group. The division in question and the Nokia Training Centre are responsible for organising training programme with the appropriate educational institute. The Training Centre and the institute organise the courses, engage the required Finnish or foreign lecturers and are responsible for the content of each course.

In addition to the normal curricula of universities and other institutes, new curricula are often needed. This is done partly in co-operation with other Nordic and European companies. These are, for example, in the field of software engineering, microelectronics and technology management.

Each post-graduate course lasts 4-5 months. Lectures and seminars are held once a week. The courses include an intensive period lasting several days, during which top international experts are invited as lecturers. Post-graduate study requirements are set by the university and professor.

Post-graduate students enrol at the university of their choice and apply for approval of their study plans. The tutor is selected and is responsible for the level of the course, its structure and content. Together with the Nokia Training Centre, the tutor shares responsibility for the approval of the course in the universities. The tutor directing the course is free to use university instructors or experts from industry as lecturers. The students themselves participate in giving lectures at seminars. A degree can be gained in three years.

During 1987 and 1988, about 40 courses were organised: The total number of students in the Ph.D. programme is approximately 200.

The M.Sc. Eng. courses consist of lectures, exercises and laboratory work. Studies follow a modular system, and students can earn a degree at their own pace. The basic subjects are specified in the university's curriculum but the student's own field is reflected in the professional subjects. Students' performance is evaluated through university examinations and a degree can be earned in about three years.

Students selected by Nokia and accepted by the university enrol in the university of their choice. Courses take place on Nokia's premises. The instructors are university personnel and the best experts from industry, both Finnish and foreign. The number of people selected for this programme is about 200.

The B.Sc. Eng. programme is conducted together with vocational schools and colleges. The courses consist of lectures, exercises and laboratory work, which at least in part are compensated for by work pertaining to the assignments. Performance is evaluated through examinations. Studies follow a modular system. The students' own fields are reflected in the professional subjects so that the courses support everyday work and career development. The number of people taking part is about 300.

Students are selected by Nokia and the technical college, which arranges subjects and sets the levels that the studies will have to meet. Courses take place on Nokia's premises. The tutors are from the institute and experts from industry, particularly from Nokia.

The first personnel training programme began at a components factory. It dealt with different sectors of component technology and quality. The result was significant interest in a wider aspect of work, improved quality and interest in studying for a degree.

The Nokia Training Centre is responsible for agreements made with the institutes and professors and other tutors. It covers expenses, including teachers' salaries and travel expenses, rents and other overheads. The students' contribution is their time and interest.

Volvo of Sweden has a comprehensive programme aimed at upgrading supervisors to managers. It has been in operation for two years and covers all supervisors in the production department. The average age of the participants is 43 years. After the one-year full-time programme the participants are placed in new positions with new requirements and performance standards. The programme is basically on company time, but requires a substantial amount of study during free time for successful completion. Volvo also has a similar programme for technicians.

Volvo has also introduced an in-company three-year industrial college. The studies are conducted in class and as practical training on a 50/50 basis. Education can be completed in three years at the industrial college, with an additional two years of practical work, after which the student may enter the final year at a technical college. After this he or she can receive an engineering degree.

Photo Courtesy Olivetti

PART II
EDUCATING YOUNG PEOPLE FOR THE 21st CENTURY

J.-P. Jallade, L. Jarenko and K. Keen

> Responsibility for solving the dilemmas of basic education in Western Europe does not reside with educational institutions alone. An increasing input is also needed from industry.
>
> Thus basic education is a major responsibility of all parties concerned: the authorities, schools and industry. It can be successfully developed only through co-operation between all of them.

In today's Europe, education is one of the most important public policy issues faced by governments. This is so because European countries are heavily dependent on "human capital" in the broadest sense for their development, whether it is to preserve their culture, traditions and ways of life, or to improve the competitiveness of their economies. No country can afford to under-invest in human capital or to reject the changes necessary to cope with economic turbulence, technological changes, shifts in social values and behaviour.

Does education prepare people to live and work in the 21st century? And, if not, what should be done about it? These are the central issues to which this report is addressed. Few education specialists, let alone parents, students or employers, would dare to answer the first question positively. Dissatisfaction with the status quo is widespread and education's performance as a supplier of a broad range of life and professional skills is often criticised. Identifying remedies to solve those problems is not an easy task, either, as intense pressures from many quarters in society converge on education.

In this context, "basic education" - meaning compulsory schooling up to 16 years of age and education for the 16-18 age group, whether it is carried out in schools, apprenticeship or in work-based training schemes - is vested with special responsibility because it is the foundation for further education in universities or recurrent learning for the rest of a person's active life. Without a good basic education, no high-level professional education can be provided and the advancement of knowledge through research is impeded. The retraining of adults to adapt them to changing labour market needs is not possible either. The strategic importance of basic education stems also from the fact that it is an experience that will be shared by most young people in the future. At present, approximately three-quarters of 16-18 year olds in the most advanced European countries are enroled in full-time schools or in training programmes which combine school-based instruction and work-based learning.

1. PRESENT TRENDS

In Europe, basic education systems usually include 8 to 9 years of general education (compulsory schooling) supplemented by 2 or 3 years of technical/vocational work-oriented education. In the past 20 years, both types of training have undergone major changes in terms of duration, scope, content, and methods, amounting to a significant revitalisation of those systems. Present priorities in compulsory schooling are:

Length: In the past, there has been a long debate about the appropriate length of compulsory schooling. The norm is now nine years - preceded by one to three years of pre-primary education - and the general inclination is not to extend compulsory schooling any further. This consensus reflects government and public realisation that, although the young cannot be adequately prepared to become good citizens and to contribute to an expanding economy in only 9 years, an extension of full-time, school-based, general education is not the appropriate policy response.

Quality: Public attention has now shifted to student achievement, with a rising concern for repeaters, late starters and slow learners. The presence of so-called "residual" groups of low-achievers and early drop-outs are the most challenging problems faced by education authorities in all European countries. Various policies, ranging from publicly-funded support for low achievers to renovated teaching techniques and information technologies, are being implemented to improve the situation.

Curriculum: During the seventies, a shift from cognitive learning to all-round intellectual and social development, stressing the socialising function of schools, took place. In the eighties the pendulum has swung in the other direction. The claim is now made that moving from instruction to socialisation may in practice endanger the learning of basic cognitive skills. The solution lies in the adoption of a core curriculum leading to minimum competencies for everybody, to which "electives" (options) that suit each child's tastes and abilities can be added.

Coverage: Although enrolment rates are approaching 100% a sizeable proportion of the student population drops out of school before completion (see Table 1). These young people leave education with either inadequate mastery of the knowledge and skills relevant to the contemporary job market, or with inappropriate attitudes and values or both. Transition education programmes aimed at improving their preparation for active life and facilitating the transition from school to work have been set up in all European countries. The EC has been actively supporting these programmes.

Table 1: Compulsory Schooling: Length and Coverage

Compulsory schooling	Sweden	United Kingdom	Netherlands	France	Italy	Germany	Spain
- starts at age:	7	5	6	6	6	6	6
- lasts for: (years)	9	11	9	9	8	9-10	8
- proportion of children not reaching the end of compulsory schooling under normal conditions	8%	n.a.	10%	10%	9% 11%	5%	n.a.

n.a. = not available

Major organisational changes in post-compulsory, technical/vocational education have taken place in recent years. The European norm now consists of a diversified system including:

- school-based streams (general, technical, vocational);
- alternance training of the traditional type, i.e. apprenticeship, and new schemes, combining school and work-based learning;
- work-based training centred on work experience and on-the-job learning.

Although the relative importance of each mode of training varies from country to country according to national traditions, a major policy objective common to all European countries is to ensure that all young people leaving compulsory eduction are entitled to at least one or two years of vocational training. In the future, enrolment rates should approach 100%. To help achieve this, the EC recently launched a major Action Programme (Enclosure 1) designed to support vocational training in member states.

The following trends in technical/vocational education can be observed:

- The share of school-based technical and/or vocational streams in total enrolments has been increasing gradually over the past 20 years, at the expense of the general/academic stream. This pattern - sometimes referred to as the "vocationalisation" of secondary education - is particularly clear in Belgium, France, Italy, the Netherlands and Sweden.

- Apprenticeship has also been revitalised in some countries: France, Italy, the Netherlands. In countries where it is well established, e.g. West Germany, it has become the dominant mode of training for 16-19 year olds.

- Linked work and training schemes for school-leavers have developed more recently. Sometimes called "alternance training" in Continental Europe, these schemes which seek to combine school and work-based learning are designed to help young people make the transition between school and work. The British YTS (Youth Training Scheme) is probably the most elaborate scheme of this kind (Enclosure 2).

- School-based technical/vocational schools are increasingly developing links with their environment. Partnerships, twinning arrangements with companies are being established. In most countries, students are now required to spend one or two months in a company as part of their academic requirements, giving rise to school-centred alternance training.

2. MAJOR ISSUES

Great things are expected from education. At the societal level, schools have important political and cultural missions. In today's European societies, nation-building is, perhaps, less important than in the past, but introducing all young people to democratic values, exposing them to a common culture, remains paramount. At the community level, schools are expected to be dynamic institutions, responding to the needs of their environment. At the individual level, not only should schools equip all young people with the right mix of general and professional skills which they need to live and work in modern, increasingly pluralistic societies, but they are also expected to expose them to a first, successful socialising experience with their peers.

Thus many pressures converge on basic education systems. In addition to all these demands, these systems are expected to operate with efficiency in the use of the vast public resources put at their disposal, and equity, that is with a concern for the less able as well as for bright students. The goal of education, which is to bring each child to the limits of its ability, remains as valid as ever. But these two constraints are not easily reconciled in practice. Removing educational inequalities is often hampered by limited availability of resources and may clash with the need for better-quality education.

In recent years, there has been an increasingly insistent demand for a closer relationship between education and working life. It comes from various quarters in society: parents anxious to see their children equipped with modern skills adapted to a changing environment, employers increasingly aware of the strategic importance of a well-trained workforce to face competition, and students themselves perhaps more conscious today than a generation ago about the role of education in the shaping of their lives. All are aware that, although schools have long lost their monopoly to other media in delivering knowledge, they remain the only structured and socially recognised route to acquire knowledge and skills.

The major issues which have to be faced by basic education systems in Europe can be summarised as follows:

General knowledge is still mostly acquired through the study of various academic subjects which are seen as goals in their own right, with little concern for interdisciplinary knowledge focussing on contemporary problems.

Curricula, meaning what is taught and learnt in schools, are too academic and schools are too slow to make the curriculum relevant to a modern society. They also experience difficulties in adapting curricula to the knowledge explosion. In some education systems, the trimming of curricula lags behind the times and children are over-burdened with traditional as well as new knowledge.

Cognitive knowledge is stressed at the expense of non-cognitive skills. Not enough attention is paid by schools to the ability to take initiative, to exercise judgement, to act with self-confidence, to work with others and to adapt to change.

Teaching/learning methods stress individual performance rather than teamwork, deductive learning through the application of theories rather than inductive learning through the practice of experimentation. Education practices continue to foster the recitation mode rather than reflective attitudes.

Concern for the **quality of education** is widespread. Attainment levels are, on the whole, rising as more young people complete 12 years of education than two decades ago. But they are not rising as fast as expectations, thus fueling widespread frustration with regard to standards of educational achievements (Enclosure 3).

A sizeable proportion of the school-age population - perhaps as much as 10% - drops out of the education system with only minimal learning achievement: insufficient reading and writing abilities, no clear understanding of the economic and social environment, little exposure to modern science. This residual group - which includes many migrant workers' children - is not properly equipped to live and work in a modern society.

The competence and commitment of teachers are vital prerequisites for producing good quality education. Yet public discontent with the performance of teachers is manifest. In recent years, the academic qualifications of teachers have improved considerably but for most of them initial training is still the only professional preparation they will ever get. Provision for significant retraining opportunities is inadequate to maintain the competence of practising teachers.

Teacher morale and motivation are often low due to poor conditions of service, low social status, unattractive salaries and career prospects. Teachers often work in isolation and have scant contacts with the environment outside school. After a few years of practice, opportunities to leave or enter the teaching profession are almost nil.

Electronic teaching aids have been widely disseminated in many schools during recent years, but their effective use in the teaching process is still marginal. Instructional television, microcomputers and videodiscs are still being considered as supplementary, add-on devices to traditional, face-to-face teaching techniques.

School organisation is often beset by administrative constraints regarding subject choices, availability of teachers, use of laboratories and equipment. Staff and resources are not always deployed optimally. The lack of administrative and financial autonomy hinders the development of modern methods of management.

The relationship between the school and the community is not sufficiently developed. Schools are still reluctant to use the community's intellectual and financial resources or to propose their services. In recent years, however, "twinning" between schools and companies have developed, leading to promising partnerships.

Education for Work

The importance of the human factor in technologically advanced economies is nowadays acknowledged by everybody. The skills and qualifications of workers are viewed as critical determinants of effective performance on the part of companies which have to invest more and more in human capital in order to maintain their competitive position in rapidly changing world markets. Hence, the heightened sensitivity of the business community to educational deficiencies. Thus, if European companies are to stay competitive, it is the duty of their managers to pay more attention than in the past to the qualities possessed by their labour forces; high quality goods and services can only be produced by a workforce with high quality knowledge and skills. And it is also the duty of basic education systems to strive for better quality teaching material and curricula, to achieve a better balance between general studies and work-oriented training and keep abreast of innovation coming from the outside world.

More specifically, current labour market trends point towards:

- a strong reduction in demand for low-skilled workers,
- universal use of modern information technologies,
- a new emphasis on transferable skills,
- a decrease in the number of manufacturing jobs coupled with an increase in jobs related to design, maintenance and marketing: according to a recent study, less than 50 per cent of the labour force in manufacturing firms is presently employed in direct production, while R&D, design, work scheduling, marketing and distribution, and financing and administration account for more than 50 per cent of such employment,
- the emergence of an elite of industrial workers responsible for automated manufacturing equipment,
- new managerial skills to reduce lead time, organise team-work and plan human and capital resources in a cost-effective way,
- female activity rates keep increasing as more and more women seek employment, but the job market is very segmented with men predominantly in industry and women in the service sectors and, most notably, in the care industry (health professions, caring for small children and aging persons). The educational level of women is rising faster than that of men.

These trends may explain why quality in education has come to be a major issue for the business community. By quality is meant everything that leads to professionalism; on-the-job professionalism is what companies now expect not only from professional and managerial personnel but from everyone, from top managers to shopfloor workers.

At the same time, industrial employment has been declining in most European countries over the last ten years. Service activities which account for 50 to 60 per cent of total employment are the only job generators. As a result of technological innovations which have been a major driving force in European industry during the past ten years, many large manufacturing companies are in a position to achieve fast increases in the level of output with a declining workforce. These trends are expected to continue in the next few years and industrial employment may actually decline because labour productivity will grow faster than output and also because the jobs created by fast-expanding industrial sectors will merely offset the jobs lost by declining sectors. Most new jobs will be in the service sector and many of them in small companies.

Thus European labour markets are caught in a double bind illustrated by an intense drive for quality as well as severe constraints on quantity. As a result, they are becoming more and more selective. Basic education systems are often criticised for their lack of responsiveness to these drastic changes. Critics are quick to assign blame to disdain for the workings of modern enterprises and to stress the many rigidities in educational institutions and structures which are held to be obstacles to rapid change. But it should also be acknowledged that many social pressures converge on schools, which have to provide high quality education for the more able as well as minimum preparation for the less able, although there may be no jobs for them.

Education does not create jobs and cannot be held responsible for the bad shape of European labour markets and the inability of European economies to generate enough employment.

Preparing young people for work is a major challenge, which can only be met through a joint effort involving schools and the business community. In modern economies, minimum thresholds of knowledge and competence are high and rising. Basic education systems should strive to prepare as many young people as possible to cross those thresholds.

3. THE THRUST OF POSITIVE ACTION

Five areas for reform have been identified. Positive action in these directions would go a long way towards solving the above mentioned problems. They are:

- Modernising curricula for professional competence
- Controlling quality
- Combining school-based instruction and work-based learning
- Teaching and learning with modern technologies
- Retraining teachers

Modernising curricula for professional competence

At the compulsory education level, the acquisition of fundamental basic skills should take precedence over other aspects of the school curriculum. Beyond traditional literacy, i.e. the "three R's", provision should be made for oral communication skills in another tongue, in English and in another major European language. Despite recent progress in this area, European education systems are not yet up to the standards required to prepare young people to live in an increasingly international world (Enclosure 4).

Systematic exposure to mathematics, science and technology, including information technologies, is a significant part of the modern literacy package which all young people should receive. But the commitment of education systems to science is uneven and not as firm as one would expect in an increasingly technological age. In the artistic, ethical and spiritual fields, stress should be put on fundamental values, common to all European societies.

At the technical/vocational education level, curricula should evolve with modern technologies and resulting changes in work organisation. Present trends show that:

- cognitive skills geared to control, maintenance and surveillance functions essential with expensive equipment, are becoming more important than purely manipulative skills;

- transferable skills, applying to various jobs in different sectors, are gaining at the expense of job-specific skills;

- social/communication skills - and this includes the ability to take initiatives and to co-operate with other individuals - are fundamental to the effective functioning of modern work organisations.

It is clear that technical/vocational education is not going to provide industry with "finished products", workers ready to get down to the job. Curricula will be of a generic nature, designed to impart the ability to acquire specific skills through on-the-job learning. Thus the building up of professional competence, i.e. the ability and willingness to make active use of one's knowledge and skills in a broad range of jobs, will be a two-step process.

Controlling quality

Appropriate assessment and certification of the skills acquired during basic education are essential to give young school-leavers a record of achievement which will improve their competitiveness in the job market. Employers also need assessment and certification to select from job applicants, to determine pay and rewards, decide what further on-the-job training they need and develop staff career prospects.

Examinations are the tool most commonly used by basic education systems to assess vocational skills. But they are better suited to assess cognitive skills than other skills, more appropriate for assessing school-based than work-based learning. Innovative principles for assessment practices are outlined below. Progress towards an improved system of assessment of vocational qualifications will lead to more efficient human resources management in companies.

Once assessed, vocational qualifications need to be certified so that they can be recognised on the labour market. Traditional certificates are insufficient to describe the range of skills, competencies and motivations acquired by young people and do not always include skills and knowledge related to new technologies.

Thus certificates should give way to profiling in the form of records of personal achievements (log book) illustrating a student's progress in each area (Enclosures 5 and 6).

The quality of education would be more easily controlled if school curricula were modularised, meaning by this the packaging of course content in sequences of self-contained learning units, which are used as building blocks towards a given level of qualifications. Modules, sometimes of an interdisciplinary nature, should supplement or displace subjects. They require clearly stated, short-term learning objectives and tightly-designed course material. They reinforce student motivation to learn and encourage self-study methods. When outdated, they are more easily replaced. And lastly, combining different modules helps customise the curriculum to suit individual student or company requirements. As modularisation in gaining ground, assessment of achievements at the end of each sequence will provide a basis for building comprehensive student records describing a wider range of experiences and competencies (Enclosure 7).

Certificates, log-books and profiles are measurement devices. They are the "currency" of the qualification market. This currency ought to be accepted on national and international markets as well. Unfortunately, little progress has been achieved towards the recognition of degrees and diplomas at the European level, but work is underway to ensure the comparability of vocational training qualifications at the qualificd worker level between the various EC countries. This is a major time-consuming task requiring co-operation among EC countries, employer and worker organisations (Enclosure 8). Work has already been completed for the following occupations: hotels, restaurants and catering activities, auto-repairing, construction, agriculture, electrical/electronic occupations.

Combining School-based Education and Work-based Learning

Many training schemes in today's Europe are striving successfully to combine school-based education and work-based learning: apprenticeships, training programmes for young people, in-company placement during the school year, etc. But the objectives of these alternance schemes vary widely. Some are mostly concerned with the guidance of young people, i.e. familiarising them with the world of work and helping them to discover their abilities and interest. These are usually of short duration, stressing social and life skills. Others concentrate on the integration of young people in stable employment through work experience. They may last from 3 to 12 months. Helping young people to secure a full-time job upon termination of the scheme is the major achievement of these schemes. Lastly, some schemes are designed to enable young people to acquire professional skills in one training occupation, as in apprenticeship. Training lasts 2 or 3 years and course content is more clearly specified than in other schemes. Skills acquired are duly assessed and recognised in collective agreements, as in the case of the dual system of vocational training in West Germany.

The Dual System of Vocational Training in West Germany

Today in Germany there is an agreed principle, upheld by employers, trade unions, the federal government and the Länder (state governments), as well as all political parties that every young person, after finishing general school education, should receive vocational training as a prerequisite to entry into working life.

This training takes place in the so-called DUAL SYSTEM OF VOCATIONAL TRAINING, which combines training programmes in companies and school-based instruction in vocational schools over an average period of 3 years. Almost two-thirds of an age cohort undergo training that leads to qualification as a skilled worker in one of more than 400 officially recognised occupations. Today, more than 1.7 million young people between 16 and 22 are trained as apprentices in this system. New training contracts average 750,000 each year.

Under the dual system trainees or apprentices undergo vocational in-plant training for four days a week and spend the fifth day at vocational school. In an effort to reinforce the systematic and theoretical part of the basic training, young persons studying some subjects have to attend vocational school for two days a week, especially during the first year.

Training under the dual system covers all sectors. The most important are industry and commerce with 45% of all apprentices, craft trades (40%), the liberal professions and public administration. The content of training is determined jointly by the Federal Institute of Vocational Training, employers and unions representatives. Training regulations are then issued by the federal government.

Training under the dual system culminates in an examination designed to establish whether the trainee has acquired the necessary knowledge and skills. Examinations are conducted by committees, which include an identical number of representatives of employers and trade unions as well as at least one teacher from the vocational training school. The overall pass rate is between 85 and 95 per cent.

The Financing of the Dual System

Instruction in vocational schools is financed exclusively out of public funds, while in-company training is paid for by the company. In 1985, companies contributed the equivalent of about 3% of total wages to vocational training.

The development of alternance training is now faced with a number of constraints, the first of which is organisational. It is not easy to co-ordinate company-based training and in-school instruction. The two sides are not yet used to talking to each other and co-operation is not always smooth. Furthermore, many training schemes are developed in isolation, on an ad hoc basis, to meet specific needs. Communication between schemes is scarce, thus preventing the development of well-signposted training routes understandable by both young people and companies. A second constraint lies in the lack of official certification in many training schemes. As a result, the skills and knowledge acquired are not recognised in the job market and those schemes are sometimes considered by young people as second-rate training. Third, the capacity and willingness of companies to enter such training arrangements is often a limiting factor, as the demand for training places exceeds the supply. At the same time, only a minority of companies are actively involved in training.

If governments are seriously interested in developing this approach, may consider the possibility of granting tax allowances to induce companies to take responsibility for training in co-operation with schools. The qualifications of in-company instructors are a key element. Instructors should not only be experienced workers and have thorough knowledge of the company but should also be aware of the difficulties and training needs of young people, as well as being capable of communicating with them and instilling motivation. Dialogue between instructors and trainees is inherently time-consuming and the former, who must divide their working life between their normal duties and their training functions, have precious little time to spare. Employers, in turn, are reluctant to allow them to spend yet more time away from their productive tasks. At present, few European companies have clear policies regarding the development of instructing staff within companies.

In the German-speaking countries, the private sector has taken the lead in organising, controlling and financing alternance training. In countries with a strong tradition of public education (Sweden, France, Italy, Spain and the Netherlands), public authorities are unlikely to relinquish their leading role, although they are prepared to co-operate more with companies by making placement periods in industry a mandatory part of the curriculum for students, and/or by setting up institutional links with industry at the school level. The French and Italian experiences are most telling in this respect.

Increasing Co-operation Between School and Industry in France

The new professional baccalaureate, set up in 1985 by French education authorities, consists of a four-year curriculum beyond compulsory schooling. The last two years include placement periods (stages) of 8 to 16 weeks in companies. About 50,000 students are expected to be enroled in this line of study by 1992. This is part of an ambitious plan aimed at enroling 80% of the age cohort up to the baccalaureate level. Early implementation reports stress the many benefits of the reform. A possible bottleneck might be companies' limited capacity to organise work placement opportunities for students.

"Twinning" operations or "Jumelages", i.e. partnerships between high schools and companies, have developed rapidly over the past five years. They consist of contractual arrangements under which both parties commit themselves to undertake the following activities:

- visits of students to companies,
- placement periods in companies for students and/or teachers,
- conferences and lectures given by company specialists to students on school premises,
- company contributions of equipment to schools,
- contractual services rendered by schools to companies.

In 1986, close to 12,000 jumelages, involving 1,200 high schools - mostly technical - were operating throughout the country. Experience shows that jumelages need time to mature: they require about one year after inauguration to be fully operational. Success depends to a large extent on the school principal's goodwill and eagerness to elicit a co-operative response from companies. Students benefit greatly from these arrangements (increased motivation at school, more realistic career plans, etc.), but so do teachers, who gain more accurate views about the training needs of industry.

Alternating Schooling and Work Experience in Italian Technical/Vocational High Schools

In Italy, various experiments aimed at integrating work experience into schooling are presently underway in about 15 technical lyceums and/or professional institutes at the upper-secondary school level. Regional governments are given a leading role in conducting and co-ordinating these experiments, the objective of which is to reduce the distance between school and work and to prepare students for entry into working life.

Thus, at the Copernic Liceo in Bologna, summer work periods, lasting five or six weeks, are proposed to students. These periods are spent with local government authorities, associations, co-operatives and less frequently in private companies. Students are submitted to the same work schedule as other workers, with the exception of half a day per week devoted to briefing and orientation with the activities of the receiving institution. They receive a small salary in the form of a scholarship. Their progress is followed up by school teachers during their work periods, when they are coached by company tutors.

About 330 students have so far benefited from these work periods at the Copernic high school and only half of student requests for work periods were met.

Alternance Training: School or Company-based?

The dual system of vocational training in Germany is mostly based on training organised by a company, on company premises and with company instructors. School-based instruction in government vocational schools is given only a minor share (one, sometimes two days a week) of training time. One may say that this is a "company-based alternance training" system which has its origins in the Medieval system of artisans' guilds. During the second half of the 19th century, industry took over the organisation of craft training which is now regulated by the Vocational Training Promotion Act of 1981.

The West German system is often presented as a model which should inspire the organisation of vocational training in other European countries. This view is faced with two major difficulties. First of all the lack of strong historical traditions often prevents companies from understanding the importance of school-based vocational training. The second obstacle is financial: training expenditure incurred by West German companies amounts to 15,000 DM per apprentice. Few companies outside West Germany are prepared to countenance this expenditure, being used to hiring young workers trained at the expense of the state in public vocational schools.

But school-based vocational education is often criticised as being too theoretical and insufficiently centred on work. Technical/vocational schools have now started to correct this by encouraging students to undergo placement periods of one or two months in industry. Under those arrangements, the bulk of training takes place in schools and company-based, on-the-job training is given a minor - but increasing - role. This "school-based alternance training" is very developed in countries with strong traditions of relying on the public sector for training, such as Sweden, France, the Netherlands, Italy and Spain.

So, should alternance training be company or school-based? There is probably no simple answer to this question. The key point is to strike the right balance between theoretical learning (at school) and practical learning. Both types of learning are important. Thus public education authorities and private companies should co-operate to develop alternance training.

Teaching and Learning with Modern Technologies

A technological revolution is coming in education. Modern technologies include here not only the already "traditional" technologies which spread during the sixties, i.e. visual aids, audio, video, but also the latest wave of information and communication technologies developed during the eighties: computers, video discs, view-data systems and interactive cables. There is a consensus that these technologies hold great potential for education. Some may fear that they will displace the oldest but still valuable technology used in education, i.e. the printed book. These fears are mistaken. The trends are towards multimedia education.

The potential of modern technologies - and especially of information technologies - can be spelled out as follows:

- They offer the opportunity for new classroom teaching methods, leading to more effective learning. Education television, computers, videodiscs will not replace teachers, they will be a "third partner" in what has been traditionally a bilateral relationship between teacher and pupils.

- They will foster a re-examination of the curriculum for basic skills, leading to integration of subject matters. School curricula stressing information-management skills will gradually become more interdisciplinary than today. With computers handling routine operations, the development of higher-order thinking skills will be encouraged.

They will introduce more flexibility in learning time and encourage self-study. Time exerts great pressure on education. One of the major criticisms that traditional classroom pedagogy warrants is that it cannot easily accommodate differences in learning rates among pupils. The whole group has to proceed at the same average pace, too slow for fast learners but too fast for slow learners. Information technology can be used to assess the learning performance of pupils, to identify gaps in knowledge and to provide slow learners with additional learning time in the form of drill and practice exercises without the presence of the teacher.

They will encourage the development of distance education, which, under the right conditions, is more cost-effective than classroom-based learning. Distance education offers great potential at the technical/vocational level to the extent that neither vocational schools nor training experiences are needed. Effective distance teaching arrangements would improve co-ordination between these two learning locations.

Finally, modern technologies are often credited with a positive effect on students' motivation and attitudes. Low motivation among students often stems from the large cultural gap that exists between what is taught at school and what is perceived from the world outside. The modern image of education technology may help bridge this gap by bringing the school and the outside world closer together, thus increasing the motivation of students. Educational technology will also increase students' control over their own learning. Such autonomy on the part of learners is a desirable goal in advanced, democratic societies because it is a first step towards the objective of learning how to learn.

A key issue that all basic education systems have to tackle is that of transforming the vast potential inherent in education technology into effective use in classroom practice. At present, three major bottlenecks are preventing full use of this technology. First, there is a cost problem. Although it has become enormously cheaper in recent years, schools have not yet acquired enough appropriate hardware. Major government initiatives to distribute computers to schools have been implemented in the United Kingdom, France, West Germany and the Netherlands, but did not go far enough to ensure that all schoolchildren are exposed to computers, for say, two hours per week. The second bottleneck lies in the paucity of good quality software suitable for classroom use. Thousands of educational software programmes exist and the standard has been improving steadily over the years, but quality is still a problem. The cost of manufacturing satisfactory software for classroom use ranges from $10,000 to 50,000 per hour, depending on the degree of sophistication required and the media used. Inadequate teacher training is the third obstacle hampering full realisation of the potential of modern technology. If investment in it is to pay off, "quick-fix" retraining of teachers for periods of one or two weeks, as has been done in some European countries, is not enough. A major effort is needed to give teachers adequate training and review staffing structures in order to provide the personnel required for smooth functioning of schools fully equipped with new technology.

Thus effective teaching and learning with modern technology require urgent action in three priority areas:

- mobilising the resources needed to ensure that schools are provided with adequate hardware
- creating the capacity to produce and evaluate courseware for various subjects,
- introducing new technology in teacher training schools to familiarise new generations of educators with their use.

Retraining Teachers

In education, nothing lasting and important can be done without a highly qualified and motivated teaching force. This obvious necessity notwithstanding, there is manifest public discontent with the performance of teachers, who often seem insufficiently motivated to fulfill the increasingly demanding tasks required by their profession. In this context, training, more specifically in-service training, offers an opportunity to upgrade the skill level of the teaching force. Because annual intakes of new teachers are very small (less than 3% of the existing practicing corps), much attention should be given to in-service training if fast results are to be achieved. Spain is a country where commendable efforts have been made in this area.

In-Service Teacher Training in Spain

Traditionally, Spanish teachers have been in abundant supply but quality has often been a problem. Since 1972, teachers in basic general education are trained in schools linked with universities. The duration of training is now three years. In the long term, this reform is expected to contribute to a general upgrading of the teaching body.

In the meantime, the Spanish authorities are eager to provide in-service training opportunities for working teachers. To achieve this, a sophisticated three-tier institutional arrangement is required:

- A network of Institutes of Education responsible for both applied pedagogical research and retraining of teachers, has been set up in each Spanish university

- The Universidad a Distancia (Open University) is also giving courses, specially designed for working teachers, in many fields of study

- Centros de Profesores (Teachers Centres) were set up in 1984 by the Ministry of Education with the support of provincial authorities in an effort to adapt curricula to the local environment

All this costs money but Spanish authorities expect it to be worth the expense if the learning achievements of Spanish children are to catch up with those of children in northern Europe.

So far, in-service training has developed in a haphazard way for various reasons. First, the supply of in-service training opportunities is uncoordinated and not geared to those teachers who need it most. Second, there is little incentive for teachers to attend courses to improve their qualifications, which are usually defined on the basis of their level of initial teacher training. No financial rewards are attached to in-service training with no effect on career development. The retraining of teachers in the use of information technologies a few years ago is a case in point. The courses were attended on a voluntary basis and teachers were enthusiastic about them, but they made no difference in their future careers compared with those who did not attend them. Third, the appraisal of teaching performance is a matter of dispute. It cannot rely on pupils' achievement alone because teachers would then be concerned only with bright children. This is why teachers' salaries in all countries are linked to seniority rather than to quality.

Little progress will be achieved in this area unless in-service teacher training is regarded as part of normal career development, i.e. as a means to gain promotion and/or salary-related rewards. It should be both a professional right and a duty. This may require that initial training should no longer entitle teachers to lifelong professional tenure, but, in the words of the OECD, "should have a specific maximum duration, after which it would expire unless renewed by a minimum number of in-service courses taken and passed." The increased emphasis on in-service training would have a number of distinct advantages:

- it would improve teacher morale and motivation by relating performance to career advancement more effectively
- it would remove the present overemphasis on "academic excellence in one subject" as the single most important criteria of teacher quality. Instead, classroom practice, and the related attitudes and personality traits, would be given recognition
- it would make the management of the teaching force more flexible, allowing people to retire from teaching in mid-career and, conversely, encouraging professionals from industry to embrace the teaching profession

The retraining of teachers in the use of information technology should be given top priority, stressing the new function and needs of teachers. To be specific, it should provide:

- basic skills to handle new technologies (computer, video-disc, etc.)
- increased knowledge of processes and methodologies of the subject
- improved skills in the area of guidance, information management
- an interdisciplinary approach to teaching, with the emphasis on preparation for work as a member of a team

The Dutch experience illustrates a forward looking approach in this area.

Training Teachers To Use Modern Technologies in the Netherlands

The NaBoNT (refresher courses in vocational education for new technologies) project was initiated by the Ministry of Education and the Ministry of Economic Affairs in 1987 for a period of five years. The prime objective of NaBoNT is to develop and distribute refresher courses to teachers in vocational education with special attention to new methods and technologies currently used by companies but not widely taught. The aim is for these new methods and technologies to be used by teachers in their lessons. NaBoNT courses reflect present and concrete demands and questions, which are addressed in collaboration with firms and with the involvement of experts from industry. When no good courses are available, NaBoNT finances the development of new ones. It is expected that every year, 5,000 teachers will take a NaBoNT course and that, by 1992, 100% of institutions for senior technical training and technical colleges will have participated.

Another objective of NaBoNT is to foster tangible co-operation between companies and institutions of vocational education. This is done by subsidising work experience periods for teachers in innovative firms. NaBoNT wants its activities to be quality controlled courses only take place if the necessary equipment is available. Activities are national where possible. Where appropriate, NaBoNT makes financial contributions to vocational education institutions that request courses. A private consultancy company has been engaged to manage the project.

NaBoNT is mainly funded by the government. It has a budget of 95 million guilders for five years. Over the first two years of operations, expenditure under NaBoNT revealed the following breakdown:

- courses: 50%
- development projects: 25%
- work experience periods for teachers: 25%

Administrative expenditure accounts for 10% of total expenditure.

4. INDUSTRY INVOLVEMENT

Industry can make a decisive contribution to improving basic education in three broad areas: defining new skills, enhancing on-the-job learning, and promoting the effective use of information technology.

Defining new skills

Industry should be part of the institutional mechanisms responsible for giving schools feedback on new developments in the workplace. With requirements constantly changing, it is essential to set up effective committees responsible for periodically updating the content of education. These committees, which should be established at the national and local level for each major family of occupations, could include industry representatives, who would also be allowed to sit on the boards of vocational and technical schools.

Such committees already exist in most European countries. In the United Kingdom, the major examining and validating bodies (City and Guilds of London Institute, GCLI, Business and Technical Education Council, BTEC, Royal Society of Arts, RSA), have set up users-providers committees where both employers and training institutions are represented. The French Commissions Paritaires Consultatives (CPC), under the Ministry of Education, have established tripartite working groups responsible for updating vocational/technical curricula and setting standards of competence. In West Germany, the BIBB (Bundesinstitut für Berufsbildung) negotiates the duration and content of apprenticeship training as well as the organisation of examinations with employers' representatives, unions and the Länder.

The quality and the effectiveness of the dialogue between education authorities and employers' representatives on those committees have improved markedly in recent years. Major obstacles that prevent further progress are:

- reluctance on the part of education authorities to entrust the committees with effective power of decision over the contents of education

- inadequate participation by employers in sectors where it is not organised effectively
- no mechanisms for following up committees' decisions by means of experimentation and evaluation

To help overcome these obstacles, one possibility could be for industry to take the lead in organising a critical review of the functions of the committees. Such a review could include the composition of the committees, their modes of organisation, the extent and nature of their remits, as well as their capacity to implement decisions.

Industry contribution at the committee level may not be enough to ensure that the right skills and standards of competence are given to young people at the school level. One way of overcoming this difficulty might be to allow "scrutineers" from industry to visit schools periodically and assess the technical quality of their teaching. The results of those visits should be fed back to school boards and committees at the national and/or local level.

Each industry could set up a small body of "scrutineers", who would be responsible for examining current practice in the teaching of a specific set of skills and systematically reporting their findings to school authorities.

Enhancing On-the-job Learning

Interest in the workplace as a centre of learning has increased markedly in recent years. Work experience is more and more valued by young people, who find full-time studies insufficiently motivating, and education authorities are attaching increasing importance to the workplace as an environment for learning.

The industry response to this situation could be organised along the following lines:

Providing **students** with work placement opportunities and/or apprenticeship places in sufficient numbers. With the possible exception of West German companies participating in the dual system of apprenticeship, most

European companies are reluctant to provide on-the-job learning opportunities on a large scale. There is still little awareness among human resources managers of the importance of these work periods in the education process. As a practical step to help solve this problem, it is suggested that companies re-assess their capability in terms of on-the-job learning opportunities that might be offered to students with a view to strengthening their participation in alternance training schemes.

Enabling **qualified workers** to become "industrial tutors". The effectiveness of on-the-job learning is enhanced by the presence of qualified tutors to help students get the best out of their periods in the company. In the British Unified Vocational Preparation Programme, industrial tutors are expected to be:

- a caring adult or in-company mentor
- a primary link or "bridge" between on- and off-the-job elements of vocational training
- a resource for advice and information, particularly with regard to in-firm project work
- a person responsible for overseeing job or task rotation and job-training; and
- someone on whom young people could model themselves as they learn to cope with responsibilities and relationships at work

These activities can be time-consuming for "tutors" who must divide their working time between their normal production tasks and their training functions. Employers are often reluctant to let them spend time away from production, especially in small companies. But this is a short term viewpoint. In the long term, the companies themselves would benefit from the presence of a body of qualified tutors capable of communicating their skills to newcomers.

Providing **teachers** with industrial experience. The effectiveness of vocational education teachers is often impaired by the lack of (recent) industrial experience. Work periods in industrial companies should be organised for teachers because this is the best way to make sure that skill requirements of companies are catered for in actual classroom practice. It is therefore suggested that companies enter into contractual agreements with vocational schools to welcome teachers for short periods of training and/or retraining. The few isolated experiments that have been launched here and there are not enough. Opportunities for in-company teacher training should be organised more systematically.

Promoting the Effective Use of Information Technology in Education

Good-quality software suitable for classroom use is not available on a large scale, thus hampering the effective use of computers and videodiscs in education. Developing software appropriate for classroom use in key subjects is, therefore, a priority, but it is doubtful that education systems can relieve the shortage by relying solely on their own resources. Industry could help considerably by using its organisational technical and financial capacity to promote the preparation of educational software.

It is customary to distinguish five phases in this work:

1) planning (investigation of the feasibility of the project in the light of what the end-product is hoped to achieve)
2) definition (detailed requirements to be fulfilled, pedagogical objectives and proposed methodology)
3) design (translation of phase 2 into technical and formalised indications)
4) implementation (transfer of the design phase into a computer programme)
5) approval and introduction (introduction and testing of the product in the specific educational environment and necessary adaptation and/or corrections)

In each of these phases, the pedagogical aspects (content and structure of the subject matter, choice of teaching tactics, etc.) have to be combined with the technical aspects (graphic design, programming expertise, composing). Teamwork involving teachers, industrial trainers and information technology technicians is a must.

It behoves industry to take the lead by proposing to set up and finance such teams in specific subject matters either in general or in technical education. The development of high quality courseware in math or physics, for instance, would go a long way in responding to industry's often-heard complaint that the teaching of maths and sciences at the basic level is not strong enough to provide a solid base for further, advanced study in engineering and technical fields. In technical/vocational education, there is plenty of scope for developing modules of courseware in such fields as electronics or bio-chemistry.

Enclosure 1

The European Communities Action Programme for the Vocational Training of Young People and their Preparation for Adult and Working Life

Council Decision of 1 December, 1987

1. A programme is hereby adopted for a five-year period commencing on 1 January 1988 to support and supplement, through measures at Community level, the policies and activities of the member States in doing their utmost to ensure, as called for by the European Council, that all young people in the Community who so wish receive one year's, or if possible two or more years', vocational training in addition to their full-time compulsory education.

2. The programme is also intended to:

   (a) raise the standards and quality of vocational training within the Community and stimulate improvements in vocational training for young people and their preparation for adult and working life and for continuing training;

   (b) diversify the provision of vocational training so as to offer a choice for young people with different levels of ability, leading to recognised vocational training qualifications;

   (c) enhance the capacity of vocational training systems to adapt to rapid economic, technological and social change;

   (d) add a Community dimension to both the supply of, and demand for, vocational qualifications on the labour market, taking account of the need to promote comparability of these qualifications between the member states of the Community.

Source: Official Journal of the European Communities, 10 December, 1987.

Enclosure 2

The British Youth Training Scheme (YTS)

The YTS, launched by the MSC in 1983, is now the most important training scheme for 16-17 year olds in the U.K. At present, it provides a structured, company-based training programme of one year's duration, including 12 weeks off-the-job training in colleges of further education, to 400,000 young people. The YTS is fully funded by the government. Its costs are estimated at £1 billion per year.

YTS is designed to provide broadly-based training in one of the 12 Occupational Training Families (OTF) rather than training for a specific job. Trainees spend most of their time doing planned work experience/on-the-job training. Most training schemes (60%) are run by private companies. The remainder are managed by local authorities, voluntary bodies and nationalised industries. About three-quarters of participating companies are small companies (less than 50 workers) in the services sector. Industrial companies account for a quarter of the total.

Over half (55%) of trainees leaving YTS schemes find full-time jobs, predominantly in administrative and clerical occupations (28%), in sales and service occupations (17%) and in manufacturing occupations (16%).

Enclosure 3

Quality in Education: Are Standards Falling?

In recent years concern for quality in education has been rising among employers, parents and teachers, leading to anxious questioning about a possible fall of standards. Some go even further and claim that standards have been deliberately sacrificed on the altar of equality of educational opportunity.

These are controversial issues because "quality" means different things to different people and interest groups. Even more, it is an elusive concept that is difficult to measure. Only cognitive achievements can be ascertained unequivocally by means of test scores but non-cognitive traits are assessed by means of "objective" indicators. Moreover, the importance accorded those traits vis-à-vis cognitive knowledge may vary among users of the system.

On the whole, however, it is not true to say that "standards are falling" in today's Europe as young people receive more years of schooling in better schools than earlier generations. Standards are probably rising but not as fast as the expectations of modern, technologically advanced companies hard pressed by international competition. Parents, always anxious to have their children receive the "best" education, also have high expectations for them and are often overcritical of the performance of the system.

Rising average standards are compatible with increased heterogeneity in educational achievements. In most basic education systems, high-achievers coexist with low-achievers and the latter, who are disproportionately concentrated among the less privileged strata of society, receive a lot of public attention. As enrolments increase, basic education systems have to cope with groups of very different abilities and motivations, thus giving the false impression that "education is not as good as it used to be".

Enclosure 4

"Internationalising" and "Europeanising" the School Curriculum

Modern industry has now become very international, with investments, production facilities and profits spreading over various countries inside and outside Europe. People working in industry are also expected to become international and school curricula may help them if they have an appropriate international dimension. In this connection, progress is required on three fronts:

- The teaching of English - the lingua franca par excellence in business circles - should start early, immediately after knowledge of the mother tongue has been firmly established, possibly in the fourth or fifth grade. At present, only Swedish and (some) Dutch children start learning English early (see table below). Pilot experiments are being conducted in West Germany and France.

- All high-school students should learn a second European language with a view to acquiring minimum working proficiency. Trilingualism, meaning by this the mother tongue, English and another European language should be the objective. At present only students enroled in general secondary education learn a second foreign language, mostly on an optional basis. Students in technical/vocational education learn only one foreign language.

- Mass media, most notably television, should support the learning of foreign languages at school by developing appropriate programmes.

- The structures of geography and history curricula should be revised to move away from the parallel study of major nations and towards presentations of geopolitical areas, with due consideration to the emergence of Europe as a political and economic entity.

Enclosure 4 (continued)

When to Start Learning A Foreign Language at School?

In most of Continental Europe, the first foreign language is still introduced in the year following the traditional primary education cycle, that is at age 10-12. This situation reflects the education structures of the past, not the needs of modern society.

The grade in which children start learning a first (I) and a second (II) language (age):	3rd grade (8-10)	4th grade (9-11)	5th grade (10-12)	6th grade (11-13)	7th grade (12-14)	8th grade (13-15)
Sweden	I[1]	I[1]			II[1]	
United Kingdom					I[2]	
Netherlands				I[3]	II[3]	
France				I[4]		II[4]
Italy				I[5]		II[5]
West Germany			I[6]		II[6]	
Spain				I[7]		

1. English used to be taught from the 4th grade, but there is now a clear tendency to start in the third grade at age 9. Because Swedish children start school at age 7, i.e. one year later than elsewhere, children in this grade are one year older than in other countries. English is compulsory up to the end of secondary school in both general and technical education. The teaching of the second language - German or French - starts in the 7th grade on an optional basis. From the 10th grade on, pupils in technical/vocational streams learn only English.
2. Most British children start learning French (75%) or German (20%) in the 7th grade but many give up their foreign language by the end the 9th grade and do not take public examinations. Only a minority of pupils, usually those proficient in the first one, study a second foreign language in the 9th or 10th grade.
3. English is compulsory from the 6th grade (last year of primary education) the secondary school diploma (13th grade) in both the general and technical streams. French and/or German are taught from the 7th grade to the 9th grade on a compulsory basis. From the 9th grade on, they become optional.
4. English (85%) or German (13%) is compulsory from the 6th grade up to the secondary school diploma (12th grade). Learning the second language starts in the 8th grade but is not compulsory for everybody.
5. English or French compulsory from the 6th grade up to the secondary school diploma (13th grade). Learning a second foreign language starts in the 8th grade but is not compulsory for everybody.
6. English (80%) or French (15%) compulsory from the 5th grade up to the secondary school diploma (Abitur). For the second language there is competition between French and Latin.
7. Spanish children start learning a first foreign language (English 70% or French 30%) in the 6th grade. Up to now, no second foreign language was taught in Spanish schools.

Enclosure 5

Basic Education Systems: How Scientific?

	Sweden	United Kingdom	Netherlands	France	Italy	Germany	Spain
Average number of weekly hours devoted to Math and Sciences during compulsory schooling							
Math (1)	4-5	n.a.(4)	3-5	6	6(6)	4-5	5
Sciences (2)	5		3	3		3-5	3
Proportion of students in scientific streams of upper-secondary general education	17%(3)	28%	58-20%(5) 30-47%	32%	41%	n.a.(7)	n.a.(8)

1) The number of hours devoted to Math vary according to grades. Only averages are given here.
2) Usually in the last three grades of compulsory schooling only.
3) This figure refers to the proportion of students choosing the natural science line in the total number of students in the 3-4 year cycle of upper secondary education. If students taking the technical line are added, the figure is 46%.
4) No data available because school curricula are not designed centrally. Not only are school principals free to decide on the number of hours allocated to Math and Sciences, but pupils also have the option of giving up these fields altogether at the age of 14.
5) The figures refer to the percentage of Dutch students choosing Math (above) and Science (below) as a subject of examination. There are two figures for each, depicting the situation in the two types of secondary schools, knows as HAVO and VWO.
6) This figure refers to the number of hours devoted to Math and Science at the lower secondary level. No data are available at the primary level as teachers are free to allocate teaching time among the various disciplines as they wish.
7) Not available.
8) The curriculum of upper-secondary education has been unified by the General Law of Education of 1970, thus providing a single route to the high school diploma (bachillerato). This route still includes two options: A (humanities) and B (Math and Sciences), but enrolment statistics in each option are not readily available.

Enclosure 6

Principles for Assessment Practices

During 1978-87, the EC conducted a European Action Programme to test new approaches to the provision of education and training to help young people become better prepared for their entry into work and adult life. In the context of this programme, 30 pilot projects across Europe were developed in co-operation with schools and vocational training institutions.

A general consensus emerged from those projects on six basic principles, which should underpin assessment practices:

* Assessment should be an integral part of the learning process. It belongs firmly within the learning process: once learning goals are established, assessment can provide the necessary feedback to students and tutors to identify strengths and weaknesses and to adjust learning and teaching strategies.

* Assessment methods should be in harmony with the ethos of the programme. It is not appropriate that programmes which aim to develop independence, initiative and motivation are assessed on norm-referenced tests of attainment which rank young people along scales from good/bad, A/D, or pass/fail.

* Assessment should be in harmony with the content of the programme. Vocational preparation aims to develop a balanced range of social and vocational skills and competencies. It is clear that assessment within these programmes should similarly focus on a balanced range of social and vocational skills and competencies. Equally, if young people are involved in active learning, they should be actively involved in the assessment process.

* Assessment should involve young people as well as staff in planning and evaluating course activities. Since young people should make decisions with their tutors on individual group or course goals, it follows they must be similarly involved in decisions on assessment - of themselves, their peers, their tutors and the course.

* Assessment should be organised in a credit unit or modular bases preferably to "end of course" assessment, because it enables young people to build up full accreditation on the basis of earned credits over a period of time.

* Assessment should have wider learning objectives than at present. Techniques to assess and certify a wide range of experiences and competencies. What is needed is a form of recording which provides non-judgemental information about a young person's experiences, competencies to be developed, abilities and achievements.

Source: Policies for Transition, July 1987.

Enclosure 7

"Modularising" the Vocational Curriculum in Scotland

In Europe, Scotland is the country which has moved most sharply away from a "linear" course structure divided into subjects towards a system of modules, usually of 40 hours' duration, accredited by a single national certificate. Modules may be taken at college or school or, for a small but increasing proportion, at centres outside the formal education system: students may study modules offered in more than one institution; credits are transferable. Courses are therefore replaced by programmes of modules; the certificate records the individual modules completed by a student. Each module is specified through a centrally validated module descriptor, the most important element of which is a list of learning outcomes.

The rationale for the modular system concerns, first, the efficient use of resources. Common elements of different courses are replaced by single modules; duplication between courses and between institutions is reduced. Second, the system is designed to enhance choice and flexibility. Programmes may be assembled flexibly from the 2,000 modules currently available; students changing their career plans, or undergoing retraining, receive credit for relevant modules already covered; the principle of credit transfer is thus extended. There is flexibility in pacing; learning may be extended over differing periods of time. The system has multiple entry and exit points; a student entering further education is not committed to completing a full course in order to receive credits; conversely, students have an incentive to build on modules they have picked up at school or on YTS (Youth Training Scheme). These points illustrate a third theme, that the modular system is intended to increase participation. Fourth, the modules provide a convenient "curricular currency" for planning the curriculum, especially in negotiation between colleges and employers or YTS managing agents. Finally, and relatedly, the modules provide a flexible framework that can accommodate further innovations in education and training, for example the need for relevant and certified inputs to YTS and the developments in work-based learning.

Source: D. Raffe and Nils Tomes, Centre for Educational Sociology, University of Edinburgh.

Enclosure 8

Council Decisions
of 16 July 1985 on the comparability of vocational training qualifications between the Member States of the European Community

Article 1

The aim of enabling workers to make better use of their qualifications, in particular for the purposes of obtaining suitable employment in another Member State, shall require, for features of job descriptions mutually agreed by the Member States on behalf of workers, within the meaning of Article 128 of the Treaty, expedited common action by the Member States and the Commission to establish the comparability of vocational training qualifications in the Community and improved information on the subject.

Article 2

1. The Commission, in close co-operation with the Member States, shall undertake work to fulfil the aims set out in Article 1 on the comparability of vocational training qualifications between the various Member States, in respect of specific occupations or groups of occupations.
2. The work may use as a reference the structure of training levels drawn up by the Commission with the help of the Advisory Committee for Vocational Training.
The text of the said structure is attached to this Decision for information purposes.
3. The work referred to in paragraph 2 shall first and foremost concentrate on the occupational qualifications of skilled workers in mutually agreed occupations or groups of occupations.

Article 3

The following working procedure shall be employed by the Commission in establishing the comparability of vocational training qualifications in close co-operation with the Member States and the organisations of workers and employers at Community level:

- selection of the relevant occupations or groups of occupations on a proposal from the Member States or the competent employer or worker organisations at Community level;
- drawing up mutually agreed Community job descriptions for the occupations or groups of occupations referred to in the first indents;
- matching the vocational training qualifications recognised in the various Member States with the job descriptions referred to in the second indent;

Source: Official Journal of the European Communities, No. L 199/56, 31.7.85

Photo Courtesy Siemens

PART III:
HIGHER EDUCATION: A EUROPEAN IMPERATIVE

M. Bylander and F. Ros

The findings of this study focus on diversity and low per capita figures for university degrees in Western Europe compared to the United States and Japan. The basic academic level of higher education is good in Europe, but low numbers of post-graduates are a striking weakness. The findings indicate a need for closer co-operation between industry and institutions of higher education.

1. SCOPE AND OBJECTIVES

The success of industry depends to a large extent on new techniques that flow into enterprises in a form of technological transfer via young graduates. Fast-changing requirements concerning knowledge, the fact that the rate of scientific and technical information growth doubles every five years and that the volume of information is 7 times greater now than it was at the end of the seventies require new efforts in education to overcome traditional and national barriers. The future depends substantially on a dialogue between higher education and industry. Critical assessments of the current system by both partners demonstrate the need to improve this dialogue. Recognising these developments, responsible institutions are reacting by pondering ways to promote higher education as a worldwide resource available on demand.

Several fundamental facts will have to be taken into account in new schemes for modified higher education:

- Universities are not flexible enough to produce, on time, students with the capacity to integrate knowledge of new technologies with their work
- Students are staying at universities too long (6-7 years)
- Today the average life of some technologies is three years
- The fast accumulation of new knowledge requires new efforts in the field of continuing education
- There is a lack of experts in information processing professions
- The strong influence of information technology in all areas is engendering new qualification profiles, so that it is possible to speak of new professions

Therefore, it is necessary to create and increase opportunities for further collaboration in this sector in order to ensure future competitiveness of the European economic system.

The main premise underlying this report is the widely held view that technological education is a key factor behind the competitiveness of

European industry, and its importance will further increase over the foreseeable short and medium terms.

In high-tech industries, there is intense global competition from North American and Japanese companies. In general, European industries are in a weaker position due both to the absence of a common market large enough to support competitive industries and to the difficulty of establishing a truly European technical community to promote technological innovation.

Although different national identities have been the conditioning factor in the development of European companies, the fact that they have been forced by the multinational groups to compete internationally in the spheres of technology and workers' skills helps offset this handicap.

On the educational side, by contrast, the systems in Europe are based more on the socio-cultural characteristics and historical evolution of each country than on industrial requirements. Thus an important gap is being created between the level of technology skills acquired by graduates and the level required for a professional job.

The speed of technological evolution and increasing market globalisation are general trends that will inevitably affect global competition and make industry's technology and resources requirements more homogeneous. Different measures are needed to close this gap. On the one hand, higher education systems must adapt to the new technological environment, and on the other, industries should have a more active role in education. In both cases, the timing of such steps and the depth of actions are key elements, due both to the slowness with which the education system responds and the need to ensure that the system does not become too dependent on the industrial environment.

Various solutions have been implemented in an attempt to solve these problems. In some cases, post-graduate courses that are more industry-oriented have been organised at university level. In others, industry has created new education centres for retraining courses. Both these solutions could be complementary and together help ease the problem.

To sum up, the main objectives here are:

* To search for educational characteristics that could help explain some of the competitive advantages enjoyed by industries in North America and Japan. At the European level, several points need to be analysed:

    - the present situation in relations between universities and industries,
    - a comparison between the efficiency of high-level technology training in different countries, and
    - possible reasons behind the lower efficiency level of European technology training systems in comparison with North America and Japan.

* A review of how the countries are solving:

    - problems of matching higher technology training systems with the industrial requirements of professionals, and
    - the need for advanced continuing education in order to update knowledge in response to rapid technological evolution and demographic trends in the most developed countries. The role of industry in higher technology training is considered in this review, as are possibilities of post-graduate training at universities and training in highly specialised centres depending on specific industries.

* To look for the best forms of action to avoid national barriers in technology training systems and build up a truly European technology community, which favours innovation and industrial competitiveness.

2. COMPARISONS BETWEEN THE EUROPEAN, NORTH AMERICAN AND JAPANESE SYSTEMS

In the table below some statistics are not mutually comparable, because countries have not agreed on definitions of terms. Teachers, for instance, are very differently defined. The relative importance of educational levels varies considerably from country to country.

Table 1 shows the number of students in higher education in Western Europe, North America and Japan, together with total population figures and number of students per 100,000 inhabitants.

Table 1. Students in higher education[1]

	Total	Students/ 100,000 Inhabitants	Population (Millions)
Western Europe	7,248,021	2,095	351
North America	14,052,259	5,178	262
Japan	2,403,371	2,006	120

[1] The terms higher education, training and teaching are used indiscriminately to refer to levels 5, 6 and 7 of the Standardised International Classification of Education used by UNESCO, which generally corresponds to the cycles which students start at the age of 17 or 18 in a normal curriculum.

Quantitative aspects worked out from the information in the 1986 UNESCO Yearbook correspond to data from the years prior to 1984.

Source: UNESCO 1986

The percentages of graduates per year in different areas of higher education are as follows:

Table 2. Graduates/Area, %

	S	C	M	T	A	O
Western Europe	50	11	17	14	2	6
North America	59	8	8	10	2	13
Japan	70	3	5	16	3	3

S = social, economic, humanistics
C = sciences
M = medicine and health
T = technology
A = agriculture, livestock, fishing
O = others

To interpret these figures correctly, one must bear in mind that the figures per inhabitant are higher for North America. Thus 14% of European graduates means only 130,000, compared with the 195,000 that correspond to North America's 10%, and 92,000 that Japan's 16% means. The figures in relation to population are 39 graduates in technological subjects per 100,000 inhabitants in Western Europe, 75 in North America and 77 in Japan.

Due to the particular interest in the running of the respective science-technology-industry systems, we have broken down the figures for graduates in scientific and technological areas into A, B and C levels (A = a diploma which is not the equivalent of a first university degree; B = a first university degree or an equivalent diploma; C = a higher university degree or an equivalent diploma).

Table 3. Scientific areas (basic science)

	A	B	C
Western Europe	7	74	19
North America	12	70	18
Japan	1	84	15

Table 4. Technological areas (applied science engineering)

	A	B	C
Western Europe	36	59	5
North America	31	55	14
Japan	16	75	9

These figures are further evidence that basic science is strongly emphasised in Europe in post-graduate studies. Indeed, the European percentage is higher than North America's, with the proviso already pointed out regarding the proportion per inhabitant.

In the technological area, a considerable increase with respect to the percentage for the A level is observed in all countries. This is logical in view of the more directly professional and applied orientation of these intermediate-level studies. The slight importance of type A training in Japan is surprising, but this is compensated for by the number of type B graduates. Where post-graduate studies are concerned, the high North American percentage and the very low European one are striking. They appear to underline a certain disequilibrium between the level of scientific excellence and the corresponding level of technology in the "Old World". This difference is of great importance since a considerable proportion of the new technological ideas developed every year in North America originate in this category of students. In Europe, on the other hand, not only is the percentage very low, but post-graduate work is also more speculative and less industrially related.

The significance of these figures is further strengthened by the appeal that the systems in the three geographical areas concerned have for students. UNESCO data indicate that the attraction of higher education in North America is more than twice as strong for Europeans as in the opposite direction (averaging over all areas of study). Furthermore, since, according to IEEE data, 55% of all engineering students in North America are from elsewhere, it appears that the attraction of North America is even greater yet.

In the context described above, the following major trends have been observed in Western Europe during the first half of the 1980s.

Despite the variety of national situations, there has been general growth in student numbers due mainly to overall growth in those less developed countries with fewer than 2,000 students per 100,000 inhabitants. Between 1980/81 and 1983/84 the total number of engineering students in the Western European countries increased by approximately 25%. There has been general growth in the number of graduates (15%), which is proportionate to the increased number of students. Taking into account the most recent figures from the CRE, the total number of graduates in engineering and natural sciences has increased and Western Europe has an advantage in absolute numbers in both fields. Relative to the size of the population, however, the proportion of engineers in the United States and Japan is still greater than in Europe.

3. FUNDING

It is significant to see what percentage of a country's budget is allocated for higher education. Of course, this figure (which is not available for all the European countries) is only a rough indicator. It covers both teaching and research and, in some countries, e.g. France, includes only a part of the funds allocated for research; in other countries, chiefly the English-speaking ones, student fees make an important contribution to the budget, but do not appear in the figures on government spending.

However, the differences seem large enough to be significant. In 1980/81, southern European countries such as Portugal, Italy and Greece earmarked a scant 0.5% of GNP for higher education, followed in ascending order, by France (0.62%) and West Germany (0.7%). Slightly more generous were Norway and Sweden with 0.76% and 0.86%. Switzerland, Finland, Belgium, the UK and Ireland spent between 1% and 1.27%, while only the Netherlands exceeded 2%. In short, the northern countries give greater support to higher education than the southern countries. The only exception is West Germany - perhaps because in a federal system much educational expenditure is independent of the central government.

That what is involved here is a statistical problem seems to be borne out by the figures for 1983/84, in which a 40% increase in the education item brings the West German budget figure up to 0.98% of GNP. This more credible figure puts West Germany on a par with its neighbours, Austria (0.98%) and Switzerland (1.01%). Some shifts were witnessed in those three years: a marked budget reduction in Ireland (20%), as well as in the Netherlands and the UK (10%), a lesser decrease in Finland, and slight ones in Norway and Greece (0.1%). By contrast, Sweden increased spending by 10% and Portugal by 5%.

Hence, we observe a certain decline in emphasis on higher education in Europe, particularly in the countries where it has been strong, such as the UK and the Netherlands - although in Britain this may be offset by increases in student fees.

Comparison with other OECD regions is difficult, owing to lack of data. Japan budgeted 0.56% of its GNP for higher education in 1980/81, comparable to southern European expenditure. On the other hand, the volume of the private sector, and student-borne costs, substantially undermine the significance of this figure as an indicator of general educational policy.

The correlation between education and research has a fundamental bearing on European universities. It would therefore seem helpful to supplement the foregoing with some data concerning research, as supplied for these years by the OECD.

As a percentage of GNP, spending on R&D increased during the 1980s. Five OECD countries spent 2% or more on civilian R&D in 1985 - Japan, West Germany, Sweden, Switzerland and the United States - with the Netherlands fractionally below the 2% mark. The share of national R&D financed and carried out by industry grew in the majority of OECD countries, whilst that funded by government declined. The role of higher education in national R&D efforts declined, although the emphasis on business sources and specifically focussed government funding strengthened links between university R&D and industrial performance. The United States maintained its position as the science and technology leader of the OECD area, while

Japan's share of OECD R&D research increased with the help of business funds. The European Community fell behind the two leading countries in terms of both R&D and share of exports accounted for by highly R&D-intensive industries.

General university funds cover the estimated R&D share of money allocated to institutions of higher education, usually on the basis of the number of students. In Sweden and the Netherlands, nearly half of all government support for R&D took this form, which explains the importance, referred to above, of higher education in relation to the GNPs of these two countries. General university funds also played an important part in Belgium, Austria, Switzerland and other Scandinavian countries (small or medium-sized countries), as well as in West Germany and Japan. All in all, the share of government R&D support distributed in the form of non-itemized general funds tended to be stable or to decline, particularly in the Netherlands and the West Germany. The share of financial and human resources devoted to research in universities declined, both at the national level and in the global R&D effort of the OECD member states. The share of university research financed by industry remained somewhat marginal, albeit increasing. All this could have the effect of re-orienting research towards shorter-term activities at the expense of traditional, basic research.

As this shows, the countries that invest heavily in research and development are, among those with similar educational priorities, the Central European and Scandinavian ones that emphasise the natural and engineering sciences. It is interesting to note that a relative decline in emphasis on the natural sciences and engineering in Switzerland is reflected by a cut in funds to university R&D. In West Germany, however, this same trend is accompanied by an increasing orientation towards science and engineering. In several southern European countries, such as Greece, Turkey and Portugal, the precedence accorded science and engineering is not matched by support for R&D.

While the dominant trend suggests a decline in emphasis on university research, linked to a general decline in the realm of higher education in Europe, the dominant countries remain those which match their educational efforts in science and engineering with sustained support for R&D, especially in the universities.

4. ENGINEERING EDUCATION

There is no specific model for engineering training in the European countries; however, a majority of them have engineering programmes on both university and lower levels. Table 5 shows the general breakdown of students in OECD countries (in %) by level of higher education.

Table 5. Engineering graduates/ISCED level

Country	ISCED level 5	ISCED level 6	ISCED level 7
Austria	7	91	2
Belgium	51	49	-
Denmark	22	78	-
Finland	32	63	5
France	10	72	18
West Germany	16	82	2
Greece	28	72	-
Ireland	37	53	10
Italy	2	92	6
Netherlands	60	40	-
Norway	44	25	31
Portugal	8	91	1
Spain	26	74	-
Sweden	25	74	-
Switzerland	30	61	9
U.K.	29	60	11
North America	37	51	12
Japan	17	80	3

ISCED level:
5 - programmes leading to an award not equivalent to a first university degree
6 - programmes leading to a first university degree
7 - programmes leading to a postgraduate university-level degree or equivalent qualification

The different models of engineering education for levels 5, 6 and 7 are presented in Table 6.

Table 6. Models of Engineering Education

	ISCED Level 5	ISCED Level 6 and 7 - engineering studies		University level	
Country	Non-university level engineering education	Type of degree/ diploma	Institutional integration with other parts of higher education system	Staff/student ratio Teaching/ research staff	All staff T/R + tech.& adm.
Austria	yes (HTBL+3 y)	Dipl. Eng.	strong	1/10	1/6
Belgium	no longer		medium	1/8	1/5
Denmark	no		strong	1/7	1/4
Finland	yes (3 y)	Dipl. Eng.	strong	1/11	1/6
France	yes (techn. super 2 y)	Dipl. Eng.	weak	1/5	1/3
West Germany	no	Dipl. Eng.	strong	1/8	1/4
Greece	yes (technologist)	Univ/Spec. Eng.	medium	1/8	1/6
Ireland	no	Eng. Degr.	strong	1/15	1/10
Italy	no	Laurea.	strong	1/18	1/11
Netherlands	yes		medium	1/8	1/4
Norway	yes (2 y)	Civ. Eng.	medium	1/7	1/4
Portugal	no	Lic.	strong	1/7	1/4
Spain	yes		medium	1/12	1/11
Sweden	Gymn. Eng.	Civ. Eng.	strong	1/6	1/3
Switzerland	yes	Dipl. Eng.	medium	1/6	1/4
U.K.	no	Char.Eng.	medium	1/8	1/4

Engineering studies are usually linked with other sectors of the institutional higher education network: "closely" linked when part of the university, as in Italy; "moderately" linked when the training of engineers is carried out in separate establishments, often called "technological institutes" or "polytechnic schools", as in Switzerland. These two models are predominant in Europe except for France, where university level (ISCED levels 6 and 7) engineering studies are generally provided by institutions (les grandes écoles) which are separate from the rest of the higher education system.

The "minimum" and "usual" duration of study in the following five fields of engineering: computer sciences/electronic engineering, electrical engineering, mechanical engineering, chemical engineering and architecture are presented in Table 7. In most countries it takes 1-2 years longer to graduate than is required by the official curriculum. It should also be borne in mind that in some countries, such as France, the real duration of study is longer if one takes into account the preparatory courses offered by specialised institutions, which provide a theoretical basis for engineering training.

Table 7. Duration of Study

Country	Computer sc. /Electron. engineering Min	Usual	Electrical engineering Min	Usual	Mechanical engineering Min	Usual	Chemical engineering Min	Usual	Architecture Min	Usual
Austria	5	7			5	7	5	7	5	7
Belgium	5	5	4	5	5	5	5	5	5	5
Denmark	5	6	5	6	5	6	5	6		
Finland	4.5	5-6	4.5	5-6	4.5	5-6	4.5	6	4.5	8
France	3	3	3	3	3	3	3	3	3	3
West Germany			4	5.5-6	4.5	6	4.5	6.3	4.5	6.5
Greece	3	3.5-4	5	5.5	5	5.5	5	5.5	5	5.5
Ireland	4	4	4	4	4	4	4	4		
Italy	5	6.5	5	5.5	5	6.5	5	6.5		
Netherlands	4	5.5	4	5.5	4	5.5	4	5.5	4	5.5
Norway	4.3	4.6	4.3	4.5	4.3	4.6	4.3	4.5		
Portugal	5	5.5	5	6			5	6		
Spain	5	6	6	7-8	3	4	3	4	6	7-8
Sweden	4	4.8	4	4.5	4	4.8	4	4.5	4	5
Switzerland			4.25	4.5-5	4	4.5	4	4.5	4.5	4.5
U.K.	3	4	3	4	3	4	3	4		

The same set of issues outlined above is found again at an international level, and advanced adult education programmes such as Euro-PACE (European Programme for Advanced Continuing Education) or university-industry training networks such as COMETT (Community Action Programme in Education and Training for Technology) must cope with all of these tactical challenges at once - a new experience for companies and universities alike. The ERT/CRE Business-Higher Education Forum, following the example of its North American counterparts, should tackle these issues from a strategic perspective, and ask itself what options are available to Europe for expanding this type of collaboration.

Such an international perspective is especially needed today, since our higher education systems are not open enough to cultural diversity.

5. THE EDUCATIONAL PERSPECTIVE

The diversity of traditions, situations and practical necessities of the different European countries will continue to maintain differences among higher educational systems. On the other hand, this has a positive aspect in that it comprises a richer source of experience. However, it would be advisable for the systems to harmonise, at least in the sense of balancing out inequalities in the quality of teaching offered and also in the sense of facilitating compatibility of qualifications and studies to permit mobility of students, professors and professionals in a European educational and professional environment. Where advances in educational methods and means are concerned, and especially as regards the application of new technologies to higher training, transnational collaboration is indispensable to achieve economies of scale.

Comparison with the North American system reveals less attention in Europe to specialisation on a higher scale (post-graduate level). This seems to be an important disadvantage, since the good basic scientific training which in general characterises European educational systems, is not taken advantage of. It would seem necessary to consider initiatives, either within the universities or in other public or private institutions to help mitigate this deficiency.

Scientific and technological changes, as well as the demand for professionals, are happening at such speed in many fields nowadays that they even produce lags during the time that a career in higher education lasts. European educational systems have shown themselves to be, in general, excessively inert in the face of these facts. It will be necessary to resort to a series of mechanisms, such as intermediate changes of stream between careers, retraining and recycling programmes for graduates, etc., to increase flexibility. Here, too, it may be necessary to complement the traditional university system with other public or private initiatives.

In spite of the fact that teacher-student ratios are generally high in the European educational systems, accelerating changes are creating deficits of professors in new areas or areas of very rapid growth. Bearing in mind the time needed to train trainers, it is necessary to launch programmes employing different means in the short-term: training abroad, utilisation of professionals in industry and incorporation of outside trainers, or residents abroad.

As already indicated, the preparation of professionals for productive activity, while not the only objective of higher education, is one of the most important. In this sense, and without detracting from the autonomy of universities, which guarantees variety and richness in scientific and cultural life, it would appear advisable in many cases to improve means of collaboration with the business world, both in regard to taking advantage of the research capacity inseparable from higher educational centres and in order to reconcile these centres' functions as both trainers of professionals and providers of social needs.

The economic spin-off, so characteristic of the North American system but of only very minor consequence in Europe, is a phenomenon very much related to the previous point. This close link between an important part of the university system and the productive system cannot be backed up only by the existence of an abundant supply of venture capital. It also needs training which both transmits the attractions of a go-ahead world and centres part of research work around activities likely to encourage a jump towards industrial adventure. Training in Europe seems, in general, to leave the individual further from that critical frontier. This could also be one of the reasons why master's or doctoral degrees acquire less numerical importance, since they are not demanded by industry so much.

6. COMPANY NEEDS

Most managers and engineers will have to work with rapidly changing technology. The actual lifetime of technological knowledge is becoming shorter and shorter. Business, industrial life and society are changing in parallel. Universities are no longer expected to turn out engineers with universal knowledge, which will serve them for the rest of their lives. They must produce flexible engineers with good knowledge of basic technology, capable of dealing with changes and new challenges.

This has to be the first step in lifelong education and training in all engineering jobs. Once people have commenced employment, it will be necessary for them to receive continuing education, in addition to the usual on-the-job training.

Continuing education will be as vital to companies as research and development, and will require a budget of the same magnitude.

In North America more money is spent on continuing education than on initial education at university level. A major part of continuing education is organised by companies themselves or by specialised continuing education institutions. In most European countries universities have been rather slow to enter the continuing education market. But shrinking public funding and increasing costs are putting universities in a situation where they have to earn a major part of their income by selling education and research services on the market. Salford University in Manchester, UK is a successful example. It is also obvious that universities cannot develop and implement continued education without close co-operation with industry.

Several initiatives have been taken to implement programmes for continuing education both in Europe and North America. Brunel University of London, the Information Technology Institute (ITI), Salford, Manchester, UK, the Society of New Professions (GNB) in Berlin, the Technological University of Compiegne in France and the University of Pisa in Italy are some examples in Europe. American institutions, active in the area include Carnegie, Mellon University, the University of Southern California. Some initiatives are also in the process of being established, like the Advanced Education Centre being promoted by Telefónica in Spain; this also aims for some action in advanced post-graduate education.

On the industrial side, large high-tech industries are very active and have introduced new video and satellite technologies in their education programmes. The real problem and possibility relate to the task of making the transition from small pilot projects to general implementation of co-operation with industry. This means, first and foremost, elimination of widespread resistance and the somewhat inflexible legal and administrative formalities that are all too common in the European high-level education sector.

It is also necessary to provide more information about and exchange experience of successful programmes already in operation. Governments, industries and universities must promote these activities. EC programmes like COMETT and DELTA have a strategic role and that is important, but it is even more important to eliminate practical obstacles to the development of small-scale continuing education.

On the <u>government</u> side it is important to

- adapt laws and other regulations to support universities and industries in developing continuing education for national needs and to promote international co-operation
- support academic staff and university organisations to enable them to co-operate commercially with industry
- be more financially generous to students in continued education courses
- increase co-operation between involved departments e.g. education, industry and communication.

On the <u>university</u> side there are barriers of different kinds

- historical - continuing education is not part of the historical role of European universities and their adaptability is by tradition limited; changes occurs almost always by addition, not by transformation

- financial - in a period of budgetary restrictions, it may be extremely difficult to cover the costs of new continued education programmes, particularly as the marketing skills possessed by universities are generally weak
- academic - university staff are often unfamiliar with planning, producing and teaching courses of the multi-disciplinary kind needed by industry

To eliminate these weaknesses it is necessary to train academic personnel for a change in attitude to continued education and adjustment to new models and contents of teaching. Some changes might include:

- make more use of modules and training materials from other institutions and universities all over Europe
- create incentives and benefits for new ideas in the continuing education process
- encourage academic staff and university organisations to co-operate commercially with industry
- be more financially generous to students in continued education courses
- increase co-operation between involved departments e.g. education, industry and communication

On the _industrial_ side it is vital to

- integrate education and training strategies into overall corporate strategies and to allocate appropriate resources
- make competence and education part of the business plan for the company
- make line management responsible for planning and budgets for the education of individuals
- provide an environment supportive of education and co-operation between university and industry in training

7. INITIATIVES AND PROPOSALS FOR ACTION

Two similar programmes have been developed by Nokia in Finland and Asea Brown Boveri (ABB) in Sweden, respectively.

The Nokia programme is based on co-operation with universities and other institutions of higher education. To meet particular educational needs, the best experts are sought either from Finland or abroad in collaboration with the institution doing the organising. Training programmes cover subjects in the fields of technology, management and business economics.

Each programme can encompass further education leading to a degree or have a short-term in-service input designed for specific training needs. Three programmes commenced in 1988. One is a post-graduate programme leading to a Ph.D., another upgrades non-graduate to graduate engineers and the third is aimed at improving the existing skills of graduate engineers. The teaching staff are drawn from universities, colleges and other institutes of higher education.

There are three integral elements of study - the individual, the company and the university or college. The programmes are conducted on Nokia's premises, both during working hours and on the employees' own time. The examinations are set by universities.

Asea Brown Boveri has developed a slightly different model for co-operation between the company and the university. Courses are given in the same areas as in Nokia's case but are designed to cover the most critical sectors of knowledge from the company's point of view rather than to lead to complete graduation.

The studies are based on "mixed days" for the students: 50% work-time and 50% for studying. The courses are designed in co-operation with the best institutions and universities in Sweden. All courses are administrated and lectures are given by guest teachers from universities.

All courses are approved by the education authorities as part of regular graduate programmes. Co-operation between the university and the company is based on a commercial commitment, which includes development, supplying courses and setting examinations. Courses last from one month to 3 years. Students receive full pay while studying. This model of co-operation has been acknowledged by the government.

The success of different projects in continuing education depends very much on how well all aspects have been prepared and on the inputs made by the student, the company and the teaching organisation. There are no standard solutions; each case is different and depends very much on local conditions. In general, however, the following features are vital:

- motivated students
- an engaged teaching organisation and interested teachers receptive to customers' demands
- a result-oriented customer
- clear responsibility on both sides
- well prepared plans with goals and limits
- very close contact between the customer and the producer

Beside this, it is important to choose an operational network designed for the specific purpose, but still flexible. In the Nokia and ABB cases the network and links between customer and producer are simple.

Figure 1: The Nokia Model

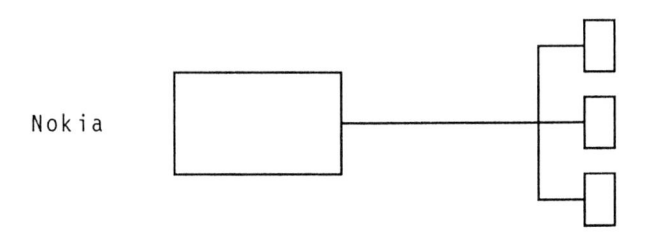

Nokia

Finnish universities

Figure 2: The ABB Model

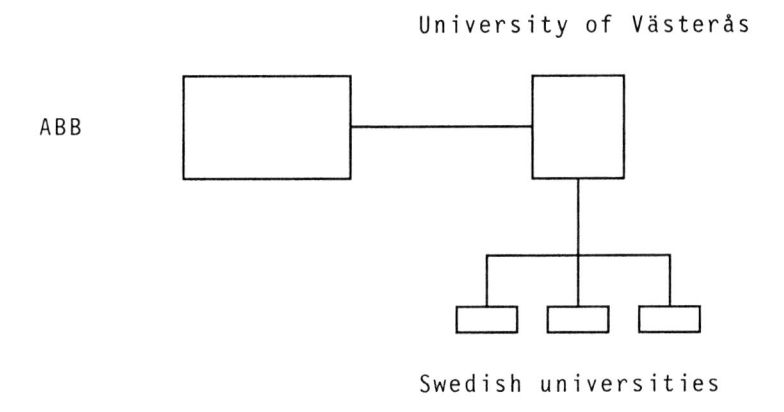

University of Västerås

ABB

Swedish universities

One customer and one or a few universities act as suppliers, the former of students and latter of teaching services and accreditations. Development, production, teaching and examinations are the final product.

In many cases the network needs a critical mass - several customers and/or several suppliers - to achieve an acceptable cost-quality ratio and capacity. Then it is very important to have a highly professional network operator responsible for designing the product, negotiating and mediating the service to all the partners. Difficulties mount rapidly if there are too many partners with highly different demands.

Figure 3: The NORIT organisation

Euro-PACE

NORIT

Scandinavian companies' partners in the NORIT organisation

Scandinavian and foreign universities

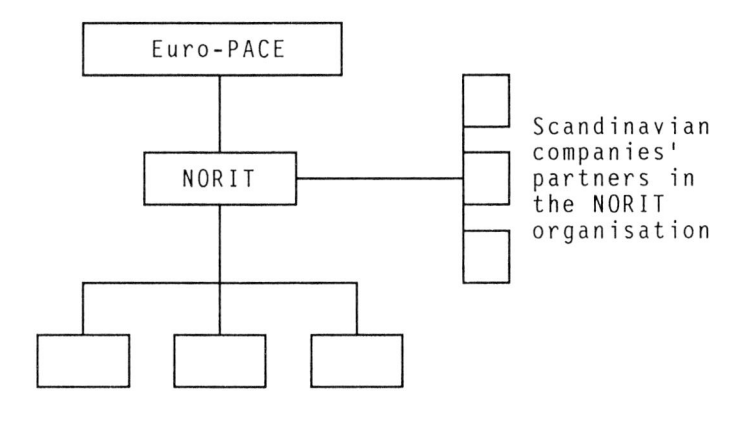

NORIT, the Scandinavian institute for information technology, is a new organisation with a network of Scandinavian companies working in the information technology area. It designs courses for its sponsoring companies in co-operation with high-level university institutions in the information technology area and functions as a link to the Euro-PACE programme.

U-link is another new network organisation close to the Swedish universities. It is supported by the Swedish labour-market organisations and industries, and closely connected to Linköping University in Sweden. A further role is to liaise with all Swedish universities in matters concerning Euro-PACE and other similar producers of high quality education programmes.

U-link is planning to establish a special distribution system for education programmes. It will be similar to the Euro-PACE distribution technique, but will use the national television network for distribution between TV broadcasting hours.

Figure 4: U-link organisation

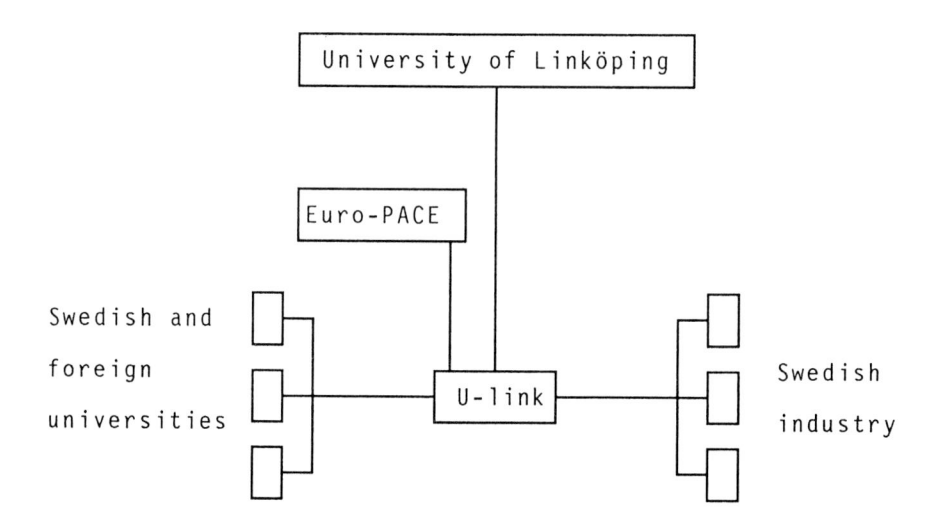

Much experience of production and distribution using this new technique has been gained in North America (e.g. NTU - National Technical University).

It would be possible to disseminate high-level education to most of the European countries in English. Small national networks of the U-link type could be linked to a large European network in the coming years, but it would first be necessary to build up the small networks in co-operation with universities and companies locally. The next step could be to link organisations like NORIT and U-link into the system and, later, switch in the other small European networks established in partnership between companies and universities in specific areas, e.g. information technology. These types of inter-European education models are possible if all communication can be done in one language, English.

If we are successful in integrating industry and university activities on a national level and then on an intra-European level, this would, in the long run, probably be the best way to homogenise higher education in Europe. To ensure this process it is necessary to start with an initiative from companies on a national or local level. A small intermediate organisation supported by industry can prepare government and education authorities to meet the new requirements of companies.

An analysis of the different higher education systems in Western Europe and the major national diversities that exist there reveals how difficult it is to consider the European countries globally in comparisons with North America and Japan. In spite of this fact, the percentage of graduates in science and technology per inhabitant in Europe, although rising, is still lower than in North America and Japan.

With these conditions real possibilities for creating advanced technology in Europe to compete with North America and Japan are very limited by the absence of the adequate critical mass of qualified professionals. This puts European industries in a weak position in international markets where they need to be competitive in advanced technologies.

Higher education in Europe is presently facing a number of acute problems. The key words here are relevance, accountability, efficiency, and the devaluation of diplomas. A general identity crisis concerning the system as a whole has thus ensued. To solve these problems close collaboration between the higher education system and industries is required in the technological field, with a more active role for industry in the education of highly qualified professionals and the adaptation of the technological higher education system to industrial requirements.

The higher education technological centres need to increase the number of graduates in science and technology, and to establish post-graduate courses directly connected to European industry requirements. In the meantime it is necessary to reinforce the role of industry in the education of professionals, i.e. to devote major efforts and capital investment to supporting technological education at universities (with long-term objectives) and to create intermediate centres and networks to train professionals (with short-term objectives).

Industry is in the best position to take action in education to improve European competitiveness by competing in advanced technologies worldwide using multinational organisations able to support activities at European level, in addition to which they are less conditioned by national environments than national educational institutions.

In order to raise the European technological level, industry has to play a more active role by supporting national higher educations systems, helping to create technological centres in each country based on the requirements of national industries, and favouring international connections to create a truly European technological community.

European collaboration programmes in R&D and education like COMETT, DELTA, and Euro-PACE could be a good way to support this educational network, but it is necessary to start by building up successful cooperation on the local and national level.

A new mentality is necessary at industrial level so that the large quantity of human and capital resources required in the technological education field can be made available.

Table 8. Age distribution of enrolments in university and non-university higher education enrolments

			Under 20	20-24	25-29	30 +	Unknown	Total
Denmark	1983	Univ.	4.1	42.1	28.4	24.7		100
	1983	Non-Univ.	3.3	63.7	22.8	12.3		100
Finland	1983	Univ.	4.8	45.6	29.4	20.3		100
France	1982	Univ. (1)	21.3	44.7	19.3	14.7		100
	1982	Non-Univ. (2)	51.5	45.5	2.1	0.9		100
Germany	1983	Univ.	3.9	51.1	31.2	12.8		100
	1983	Non-Univ.	29.8	40.3	12.8	2.1	15.1	100
Greece	1981	Univ.	30.3	52.7	9.4	4.1	3.5	100
	1981	Non-Univ.	54.7	41.0	3.0	1.3		100
Ireland	1983	Univ.	45.3	45.5	5.3	3.9		100
	1983	Non-Univ.	36.3	46.6	9.1	8.0		100
Netherlands		1983 Univ.		13.3	47.6	24.6	14.5	100
	1983	Non-Univ.	17.0	44.0	15.8	16.3	6.9	100
Spain	1981	Univ.	25.4	49.7	11.1	7.5	8.1	100
	1981	Non-Univ.	28.4	43.9	9.8	2.4	15.4	100
Switzerland		1983 Univ.		15.5	50.3	21.8	12.4	100
	1983	Non-Univ.	6.5	53.6	23.0	16.9		100
U.K.	1975	Univ. only (1)	39.5	53.9	4.1	2.5		100
	1981	Univ. only (1)	34.7	45.7	8.6	11.0		100
USA	1981	Univ.	24.1	40.8	14.5	20.6		100
	1981	Non-Univ.	32.9	29.6	13.2	24.3		100

(1) Figures refer to universities only and not to all university type higher education.
(2) Includes only the IUT's (Instituts Universitaires de Technologie).

Source: OECD Education Statistics

Photo Courtesy Fiat

PART IV
VOCATIONAL EDUCATION ACROSS EUROPE

A. Chaplin, C. Hayes and H. Lemke

> The general trend is towards using vocational education and training primarily as a tool to solve short-term, often production-related difficulties. VET should be brought closer to the concern of top management and treated as an investment for the future prosperity of the company in the long run.

1. INTRODUCTION

The most vital asset that Europe possesses in meeting competition is the brains and trained hands of its people, who work and produce in its factories and offices. Improving the competence of this asset is a responsibility that cannot be ignored.

Companies are keen to prevent their operational capability from being impaired by people inadequately prepared for the tasks which need to be done. Training for this purpose is therefore of high priority.

Most companies are aware that short-term market responsive training alone is not enough. Its exclusive pursuit merely becomes a constraint on commercial strategies. Thus there is a need for complementary VET policies with have longer-term aims.

Long-term approaches have several characteristic features:

- training to enable the workforce not only to adapt to change but to participate in it; i.e. overqualification to maintain a flexible workforce with broad competence

- long-duration initial training, which provides a basis for brief further adult training periods when required

- in countries where apprentice schemes or some other form of general youth training covered almost all young people, companies strengthened and often expanded programmes of this kind

- active participation in a national qualifications strategy and support for regulated schemes with national minimum standards

- long-term VET orientation linked with the strategic aims of the company, its strategic planning and personnel development

- a central VET budget for achieving longer-term aims; with line managers and units spending what they consider necessary for additional more immediate purposes

Short-term approaches are characterised by the following features:

- using flexible training systems to respond to pressing day-to-day priorities

- ensuring the capability to react quickly, by training workers in skills which are needed; or will shortly be needed as a result of changes in production or service requirements

- those responsible for training are close to, and respond to the wishes of their line managers and business units

- programmes which train people to perform specific sets of tasks well and handle specific types of situations

- dispensing with apprenticeship or other long-term VET

- hiving off VET as an independent cost-centre or a separate business

- short-term responsive training as a means of minimising training costs

The trend is towards a growing pre-occupation with short-term policies. In part this is a reaction against the remoteness of longer-term training aims, "they don't respond to today's needs", as a closer integration of training with what goes on in the business. However, a desire to minimise costs undoubtedly outweighs these motives.

An excessive concentration on either long-term or short-term VET is detrimental to the interests of companies. It is more appropriate for them to pursue simultaneously both long-term VET policies in order to develop a workforce with strategic capability and short-term ones to achieve the necessary flexible market responsiveness.

Survival and profit require people who can follow instructions correctly and manage situations effectively. When a workforce has to adapt to new demands, the absence of a sound fundamental grounding becomes a handicap. This is especially noticeable when a more positive, creative contribution rather than mere compliance is asked for.

Industry increasingly needs a strategic capability, which comes from people with the kind of knowledge, skills and understanding that can best be acquired through solid and substantial learning experience. Given a sound base it is much easier and cheaper not only to add and update competence but also to learn positively from experience, accept greater responsibilities and make creative contributions.

VET is one of the critical success factors in the successful implementation of strategies and business plans. For this reason alone, the widely practised convention of treating VET expenditure as a cost rather than an investment must be rejected. The capability of a company becomes a prime asset, and an essential prerequisite for success.

The main emphasis of VET policies and activities is on further training and retraining of adults rather than on initial training. Little support is given to non-job-related education. Within further training, courses for adaptation and updating are more prominent than courses for upgrading or promotion.

While these developments are virtually universal, there is a clear divergence between practices in the sphere of initial training. Some companies provide long duration initial training on a regular basis. Others have abandoned this and rely on retraining their existing labour force. Where it is necessary to replace workers lost through retirement or other causes, or where the workforce is growing, trained workers are recruited from outside. These recruits are given short induction training only or are expected to learn on-the-job.

The trend is to recruit virtually no untrained or unskilled workers. Young workers emerge from initial training at 18 in those companies which continue to provide it, or adult workers are recruited.

A further trend regarding the training of non-supervisory workers has been observed. Measured as a proportion of expenditure for all adult training, the largest share at group corporate level is devoted to management training, and at operating company level to technical training for people who are already qualified and experienced.

2. INTERACTION WITH THE PUBLIC VET SYSTEM

Companies are frequently critical of the public VET system, although there is a general view that public institutions are markedly improving. The degree of satisfaction and dissatisfaction appears to depend strongly on the level of involvement of the company concerned.

Companies can obtain what they want, but not without input and collaboration. The interdependence of company VET and public services is frequently seen as a positive factor, which benefits the company if the two sides work together. Industry wants high standards of basic education and training from public institutions.

Company responses revealed that there is no support for the development and implementation of European VET policies. Even individual companies do not, as a rule, impose common VET policies on their operating units or subsidiaries in other countries.

3. STRATEGIC CAPABILITY AND FLEXIBLE RESPONSIVENESS

In response to uncertainties and market pressures, many companies are aiming to make training more flexible, respond more rapidly, grasp short-term needs, be more cost-effective and minimise costs. At the same time there is a widespread desire to identify and support long-term human resource development needs, adopt a long-term orientation and link VET with the company's long-term strategy.

In this regard, companies pursue a wide spectrum of practices. Some are closer to the end of the spectrum, in which flexible responsiveness is the overriding priority, with little real effort being devoted to building strategic capability. At the other end, there are companies which devote considerable resources to long-term VET policies. It is more common for such companies also to favour short-term VET programmes.

Whether it is a question of being unable to accommodate as many newcomers as before, or simply of not being able to find them, the result will be the same: the workforce will largely consist of people already employed by the company.

Additional formal training or retraining is inescapable when work is subject to considerable change. Few companies have developed workforce planning to the extent that they can anticipate the number and types of occupations in which change will necessitate training.

Further training in most companies is oriented towards short-term needs, with little provision to retrain or to further train a certain quota of employees every year.

4. NEW OCCUPATIONS AND TECHNOLOGIES

In terms of future vocational competence the criteria most frequently mentioned are new occupations, new technologies, and flexibility. However, when one looks into VET programmes in detail, it is obvious that only minor changes have been made or a few new elements added.

New technologies alone are by no means sufficient to facilitate independent long-duration training programmes. The curricula of some recent training programmes in mechanical, electronic and electrical engineering in West Germany demonstrate this.

It is clear that training programmes have to take into account the latest production training and service processes. Subjects commonly pointed to include:

Modern technology, e.g. transition from mechanical to electronic data processing, automation, environmental technology, integrated circuits, production methods and new materials.

Office and administration works, e.g. office automation and word processing.

Teamwork and co-operation, e.g. communication skills, languages, flexibility and adaptability.

New corporate philosophy, e.g. life-long learning, corporate culture, communication and social training and business awareness, and **quality and service**

5. SKILL SHORTAGES

Although company training policies would need to be designed to cope with shortages, this is rarely the case in practice. Shortages of vocationally and technically qualified people are particularly acute in those occupations and specialisations that can best be learnt through company-run courses.

This problem is most acute at highly skilled levels and where new technologies and materials are involved. Such categories include mechanical engineers, computer, electronics and communication experts, and software engineers. Companies obviously want people who are not only trained but already experienced as well.

The problem is not universal, but strongly dependent on the business sector. It is therefore important to establish linkage between company training policy and identified shortages. In most companies, training for blue collar workers already in employment is only provided on the basis of need.

What is to be done for older people who have worked for many years in clearly defined, limited and sometimes rather repetitive jobs? This is one of the biggest challenges that human resource development must meet.

There are two ways of looking at it. The first is to examine how urgent the need is to develop their skills and whether it is worthwhile investing in such development. The second is to examine what goals the programmes would have. Should they be aimed at developing competence or should they include development of the company culture, a feeling of belonging and a commitment to common company goals?

VET systems meeting the demands of the future will have to feature two aspects of **responsiveness**: on the one hand, employees capable of responding to new demands; and on the other, a responsive training system.

This means giving employees the training they need to respond quickly to company needs, which in essence would be overqualification, but also a training system that responds quickly to current needs. However, a tendency to become too exclusively preoccupied with short-term VET is an inherent danger in the latter kind of system. Responsiveness is thus most often interpreted in a short-term context, but it is recognised that training of all kinds is by nature preparation for the future.

Training is not seen as an end in itself but as a means to reach company goals. The orientation of training has been recognised as just as vital to competitiveness as customer and environment orientation.

An orientation towards the lowest level of immediate needs can be perceived in the training activities of many companies. There is a growing dilemma as to whether the prime objective should be to make the workforce capable of meeting changing and more demanding customer needs or to train for short-term identified tasks only.

Where costs figures are available, the bases vary, thus making comparison difficult. Most company head offices make it a policy not to intervene in this area. They prefer to leave the running of VET, including budgeting, to their line managements.

Only few companies have a central budget for VET. In some, however, head offices show a keen interest and may even influence the budgets of individual units. Where this is the case, investment in initial training is greater than in other companies.

Companies which themselves provide initial training for their new recruits do not consider themselves at a disadvantage compared with others who rely on initial training provided by public institutions. On the contrary, they see their own training as a formula for success.

Informal Training or learning by doing a regular job is by far the most important way of developing skills and competence. But no matter which training mode is adopted, formal or informal, the benefits and opportunities are not evenly spread among all employees, but biased towards higher levels. If no measures are taken to rectify this, major disparities between different groups of workers will arise.

If schools were to attempt to meet industry's requirements, they would have to become more specialised and customer-oriented. But the customer (a company) can provide jobs for only relatively small numbers of students. Meeting specific requirements would lead to much earlier decisions on individual students' careers as well as to agreements between companies and youngsters on their later recruitment. A pilot scheme to try out these ideas has been launched in Britain.

There is a more basic contradiction between the provision of broadly-based skills and competence and the need for industry-specific specialisation. Students are reluctant to embark on a narrowly-defined career path at an early stage, and companies also prefer individuals with a well-rounded educational base, from which later specialisation can grow.

6. STRUCTURES AND ORGANISATIONAL PREFERENCES

Companies recognise that appropriately educated and trained personnel are a major asset. Providing such a workforce is a major objective of their competence development policies. However, their VET activities in practice and the results of their policies vary widely.

Head offices are much more directly engaged in management training, especially for top executives, than in VET. That is not to say that they are unconcerned about competence development at lower levels, but since they leave it to management, they have no detailed information on what is happening in units remote from themselves.

The **funding** of VET is decentralised in nearly all companies. Individual business units have to pay for it, usually on a real cost basis, even if it is provided by the same company or corporation. This is generally done by charging internal fees per course or participant. There is usually no corporate budget, except for overheads (in some cases) or for really special programmes, e.g. new technologies.

A clear exception was one company, which is a leader in its technology and products. It has training budgets at the head office and unit levels. The training needs of programme participants are determined jointly by line managers and the training department, but paid for out of the budget of the latter. Thus the company ensures that the amount of training that is strategically required is in fact provided.

There are only a few cases in which companies receive external funds to finance or sponsor their own training activities. There are also a few levy and grant schemes, but companies do not regard them as an appropriate solution.

Nevertheless, most companies try to avail of all available national and regional funds and programmes. In some companies the training unit sells its services to external clients. There is no indication that companies with the opportunity to find finance for substantial parts of their own programmes have more extensive training activities than others.

The **reporting structure** reflects priorities in training policy. As a rule, only management training and some staff training need be reported on directly to head office. Technical and vocational personnel report to line managements.

Decentralisation is the in trend in modern company policies, and training is no exception. In line with this, the function of many training units has been changed. Their role has also changed; instead of carrying out training they now organise it. The majority of central units no longer provide training, but act as internal consultants providing a service to other units. The new function of these centres involves mediating information about training opportunities both inside and outside the companies.

Decentralisation, however, has implications not only for training units. All managers are responsible for developing the competence of the people who report to them directly or indirectly. In the new approach, these responsible for training are not just expected to define what skills are needed, but also to see that they are imparted and developed. A consequence, however, can be that managers tend to make short-term decisions, leading to a lowering of the level and scope of training. Companies do not usually provide training opportunities which are not in line with their own needs, although some organise comprehensive general education programmes open to all their employees.

Ultimate **responsibility** for the development of competence resides with the individual, who must be willing to contribute the interest and effort. Management's role is to provide the opportunities and encouragement.

7. MAKING EDUCATION AND TRAINING A BUSINESS

Some companies are abandoning their long established training units or restructuring them totally. The alternatives that they have chosen include buying services from external institutions, or setting up external and independent institution as independent profit centres and buying services from them. In the latter case the institutions not only serve their parent companies but also sell training to other companies, governments and individuals. In cases where training units are made independent profit centres there is a trend to link consulting with research and training.

Linking VET more directly to company strategies is a common objective in many new approaches. In many companies expansion of training activities and reorganisation of company VET units are being done at the same time. One interesting question that remains open in this respect is whether reorganisation created expansion, or whether it is merely a means of handling expansion in the most economical way. It is clear that one thing the new approaches have in common is a desire for minimisation of costs.

Many companies believe that training becomes more related to their needs if it is not externally regulated. With a view to greater flexibility, they have gone for de-regulation and changed their internal vocational training programmes accordingly, even for initial VET. Yet, other companies have relied increasingly on externally regulated apprenticeships and there is nothing to indicate that they have suffered a disadvantage as a result. On the contrary, externally regulated schemes have proved to be very flexible internally, thus allowing companies to adapt continuously. Furthermore, a regulated scheme designed to guarantee a certain minimum level of competence nearly always involves a greater breadth of training, benefitting not only the company but industry as a whole.

However, building organisational capability on the lowest acceptable level of basic competence may undermine future growth and profitability.

The study was not designed to elicit detailed information on pedagogical in-company methods, which would be useful for training experts. The examples below confirm that companies are not so much striving for fundamental reforms as making the best use of existing systems.

Supervisor to Manager - Volvo - Sweden

A comprehensive programme intended to develop supervisors into managers has been in operation for two years. It includes all supervisors in the production department. The average age of participants is 43.

The one-year full-time programme is entirely on company time, but also requires supplementary study outside normal working hours. Participants are updated in technology, mathematics and management techniques.

Competence Development Programme for Blue Collar Workers- Volvo - Sweden

This programme started with a survey of all blue collar workers to inventory their skills and the work they actually do.

After this, the workers were offered individual made-to-measure training programmes on company time. The response has been very positive. Company plans now include programmes for the next few years for approximately 75% of all blue collar workers in all age groups.

Linking In-Company Programmes with the Public Scheme - ABB-Sweden

The company, in co-ordination with local state schools, has introduced various additional, general subjects from the syllabus of upper secondary technical schools. These subjects are taught on company time.

On completion of their courses, the apprentices/students may decide to work in the company or re-enter the public system of education to progress further and obtain higher qualifications.

Qualified Production-Process-Operators Training - Pilkington-United Kingdom

Arranging formalised training for process operators has always proved to be a big problem. After about one year of basic training - mainly benchwork and machining - there has usually not been enough content to justify another two years of formalised VET, as is the case with, for example, engineering, machining, or electrical craftsmanship training. As a substitute for well-trained production-process operators, many companies have employed people who have been trained in other occupations, principally engineering, mechanics and other crafts. In these conditions it has never been very attractive for capable young newcomers to go directly into a production job.

Against this background, Pilkington has decided to train newcomers directly in a three-year production-processing scheme. It includes one year off-the-job basic training, almost identical with the training of craft workers in engineering. Subsequent training specialises in production aspects. Most of the training from the second year onwards is on-the-job instruction to a tightly controlled syllabus. The objective of the scheme is not only to produce highly skilled production operators but also to identify and prepare potential supervisors for production.

Top-Level Apprenticeship

In the past, and for many people still today, apprenticeship has had the image of a training scheme that is principally, if not exclusively, designed to impart manual skills to young people who have completed their compulsory education.

The following examples indicate a development towards top-level apprenticeship.

Apprenticeship for more highly educated people

In the 1980s, apprenticeship has become increasingly attractive to young people who have completed more than just their compulsory education. That includes those who are entitled to go to university or other higher level institutions. This is not only the case with occupations that demand and attract highly educated applicants, such as banking, industrial and commercial administration, electronics and chemistry. It also applies, though to a lesser extent, to the majority of occupations for which recognised training schemes exist. Today the majority of those starting an apprenticeship have achieved more than compulsory general education, whether in general streams or in technical, vocational or commercial schools.

Apprenticeship plus

For these programmes companies select applicants who have had general education to at least the upper secondary level.

The programmes generally follow regulated training schemes and cover the regular apprenticeship programme, but are implemented in a shortened, compressed period of time, together with additional training related to a broader technical or business field.

Tertiary level apprenticeship

These programmes include regular apprenticeships, and are company-based, although arranged jointly by companies and university level institutions.

On completion of a programme the student/apprentice has reached a level similar to that of a graduate, in addition to acquiring the skills and competence of somebody who has succeeded in apprenticeship.

8. COMPANIES AND THE PUBLIC SYSTEM

The diversity of environments in which companies operate is illustrated by the following examples:

- A dual apprenticeship scheme, as in Switzerland or Germany. In this companies play the decisive role.

- Schemes where VET is primarily offered by public or semi-public training institutions. In this system companies provide a substantial part of the programmes.

- Schemes in which VET is totally the responsibility of schools.

These systems exist side by side in some countries. Some companies provide only orientation stages for students in technical/vocational schools. There is hardly any case in which companies arrange for the type of training that is given in schools. In other words, the situation is always characterised by a certain fundamental job sharing between systems.

Company participation in VET depends on commitment. Those with a record of high quality education and training are most satisfied with the public system. Most companies are satisfied with the current level of industry representation in schools on VET matters, at all levels from planning to implementation. Weaknesses in the performance of public VET are in part a reflection of faults in the way companies play their role.

Companies' assessment of public VET could be crucial in the development of a common strategy. Instead of trying to describe how companies see the public systems in detail, a few typical statements made by companies during the course of the interviews will suffice.

> "Of course we could suggest changes on everything, but basically it is O.K."

> "The school system in itself is O.K. but the curricula are old and the equipment is old. The system should be changed at the same speed that industry changes." However, the same interviewee said "Schools can't be flexible enough to adapt to change in the country".

> On whether the public or semi-public systems of VET react in time to changes in business needs: "Of course not, but that is not something really worrying".

> "If we really expect schools to do all the things we want them to do, that would become very expensive, in fact exorbitantly expensive. So we have to do many things ourselves". And: "We find what we want on the market. If we can't find it, we build it ourselves. There is no shortage."

On co-operation with schools:

> "If the company starts this activity, teachers and authorities are very interested, but the initiative must come from the companies." And: "Industry should go to schools, not wait to be invited".

VET policies have to be both strategic and operational in nature. They require the participation of the highest levels of company organisations. Pursuing both long- and short-term policies will ensure the development of a workforce with a strategic capability.

The training and education of non-supervisory/non-managerial workers needs greater effort and greater investment of money and other resources.

Photo Courtesy Carlsberg

PART V
MANAGEMENT DEVELOPMENT PRACTICES

W.A.G. Braddick, D. McAllister, J-P Paul and G. Testa

Management development is becoming more business driven, action-led and practice-oriented. There is a clear drive towards "Europeanisation" and internationalisation. There is a need to take steps to bring the opportunity for management development to a wider population.

A European management model specifically catering for the requirements of the single market after 1992 is emerging.

Although management development has recently expanded rapidly, there remain many differences, anomalies and obstacles remain to the development of a European training system which will ensure equal opportunities and common standards.

1. EUROPEAN MANAGEMENT EDUCATION

Although the system of management education in Western European countries has evolved in a variety of ways, there are common features. In the late 19th century most European universities remained reluctant to recognise management as a legitimate subject of academic study . Although some, like Birmingham University, established a degree in commerce at the turn of the century, in most European universities management was taught (if at all) as an adjunct to more "respectable" subjects like engineering (in the United Kingdom) or economics (in West Germany). In most European countries, it was the technical colleges and commercial schools which initiated studies in business and management - a tendency which is still reflected in the British Polytechnics, the Fachhochschulen in Germany and the Ecoles Supérieures de Commerce in France - to give examples from the larger industrial countries.

Major growth in management education and development in Europe took place after the war. The industrial and commercial achievements of the United States were widely admired and became an example for the reconstruction of post-war Europe.

The late fifties and early sixties saw a veritable explosion of management education institutions in major European countries, most of them modelled on the business schools of the United States. In Belgium the Fondation Industrie-Université, created in 1956 through the co-operation of business and the universities, was founded to foster management education at the university level. As a result, eleven out of the twelve Belgian universities offer the opportunity to study management. In Britain, the Foundation for Management Education performed a similar function in the early 1960's to bring the first British business schools - London and Manchester - into existence. In France, the Ecoles des Hautes Etudes Commerciales (HEC), the Ecole Supérieure des Sciences Economiques et Commerciales (ESSEC) and the Ecole Supérieure de Commerce de Paris (ESCP) created early in this century form the core of the present Chapitre of sixteen French "écoles de gestion" set up in 1985 to ensure the quality of education practised by its members and to promote the status of their diplomas. It is the Chambres de Commerce which have traditionally provided the drive and financial resources to create and develop this system, which produces the elite of French management. In Spain, Italy, Holland and the Nordic countries, a similar pattern of business schools was established, often on private initiative, in the 1960's and forms the major source of trained managers. Two of the best known schools in Europe which have recently announced their intention to merge, the International Management Institute Geneva (IMI) and the International Management Development Institute Lausanne (IMEDE), had their origins as company training centres. IMI was founded in 1946 to serve the needs of Alcan Aluminium Ltd. and IMEDE in 1952 to provide a similar service for Nestlé S.A. The European Institute of Business Administration (INSEAD) at Fontainebleau was also founded privately in the late 1950s.

Management studies have now rapidly expanded throughout the university system and in France, Britain, the Benelux countries and the Nordic countries most universities now offer MBA type programmes. Southern European countries still rely similarly on the private system and Germany has shown no interest in this type of education at all. One business school exists there.

Executive development

The origins and evolution of executive development activities reflect similar influences to that of post-graduate education. Before the outbreak of the Second World War, most European countries paid little attention to the development of practicing managers. It was either believed that "managers are made" or that they could learn the skills informally as part of the development of the job.

Post-war Europe admired what it found in the United States. Productivity missions were impressed with the efforts which were made to train mature managers on the other side of the Atlantic and the war itself had drawn attention to the importance of management and leadership, as well as being the forcing ground for developments like operational research techniques which have a direct application to industry and commerce.

As a result of these influences, centres were established either by employers' associations - like De Baak in Holland, the Swedish Management Group or the Kursusejendommen Bogehoj of the Danish Employers' Confederation. In France, the main drive again came from the Chambres de Commerce. In Britain, Henley Management College and Ashridge Management College were set up as private foundations initially funded by industry and commerce in the late 40's and 50's respectively. Two of today's pre-eminent business schools, IMI Geneva and IMEDE Lausanne, originated as company training centres, and in the heartland of Europe many of today's pre-eminent international companies undertook (and undertake) extensive in-house training programmes for their own managers. Companies like Pilkington, Plessey, Philips, Volvo, Olivetti, Pirelli, Fiat always invested heavily in management development activities. Fiat for example created a separate company (ISVOR-FIAT) to undertake its training activities. This is even more true of West Germany, where currently only one purely German business school exists. West Germany relies on an extended apprenticeship system to train its managers based on systematic practical training combined with well developed systems of internal programmes.

Currently, the system is going through another phase of expansion. The demand for management education and development in all Western European countries and at every level from under-graduate to post-experience is growing by leaps and bounds. The demand for business studies at undergraduate level now represents the highest number of applicants in any faculty in many European countries. Often the quality of students is also very high. The demand for MBA courses is such that many schools are significantly increasing their intakes and "invaders" from the United States are offering programmes in Europe, whilst private institutions are also taking the opportunity to develop new approaches. Distance learning institutions also offer MBA programmes. A similar pattern is clear in the executive development field. In response to the very large increase in demand, many newcomers - particularly consultants - are entering the field and a wide range of pedagogic methods are being introduced.

The similarities then are clear. As far as generalisations can be made, the management education system originated outside the university system, although the universities are now very active in the field. Management development is essentially a post-war phenomenon, concerned with the creation of a managerial elite. Even taking the recent expansion into account the number of managers who receive any formal training at all is a very small proportion of the total managerial population in most countries.

A major difficulty in making comparisons between the European countries in the management education and development field, or even in assessing the efforts in a particular country, is the lack of adequate data, exacerbated by the fact that systems differ so widely. For example, it was alleged until recently that the United Kingdom fell far behind its competitors as far as investment in industrial training is concerned. But figures produced in the Oxford Review of Economic Policy (Autumn 1988) suggest that industry spends £144 billion per annum and the Training Commission an additional £3 billion per annum. The total adds up to 7.8% of GDP - about the same as Britain's major competitors.

Similarly, although it is possible to compute the numbers of those attending university degree courses (although these are often not strictly comparable), there is no systematic data on the training of experienced managers and very little evidence about the amount of in-company training undertaken in a systematic basis. The provision of an adequate data base on European management training would enable a much more systematic evaluation of the differences between countries to take place.

There are, however, significant differences. The West German system of management development is the best example. Future managers are trained at universities and Fachhochschulen in studies like business administration, law or engineering followed by a prolonged period of on-the-job learning supplemented in the large companies at least by an extensive range of internal management development programmes. There has never been any demand to create business schools. The traditional apprenticeship system is thought to produce the best managers.

Differences also exist between the intake of graduates into managerial posts. In Britain only 24% of top managers are graduates compared with 65% in France and 62% in West Germany. This is partly a reflection of the fact that only 14% of 18 year olds enter higher education in Britain compared with 40% in France and West Germany. Similar disparities can be found between the provision in the heartland of Europe generally and

Southern Italy, Greece and Portugal, which are still under-provided with facilities for the development of managers.

There are also major differences in the sources of recruitment of managers. For example, Britain has 12,000 qualified accountants compared with 4,000 in West Germany. On the other hand, West Germany has a very high proportion of lawyers in senior management compared with its neighbours. In West Germany, entry into business is at a much later age than in the U.K. (28-30 years old compared with 22 years), and training within industry is much more systematic than in other European countries. Higher standards of mathematics are demanded of those who study management in France than of their counterparts in the U.K. for example.

There are geographical contrasts. Northwestern Europe has a generous provision both of business schools and executive development centres. Scandinavia, the British Isles, the Irish Republic, France and the Benelux countries not only have an extensive network but it is growing rapidly and in Britain, parts of Scandinavia and Holland in particular, distance learning is extending the ability to study to a much wider population. On the other hand, managers in Latin countries have much less choice. It is true that there are outstanding business schools in Spain and Italy and in the latter country in particular some large companies have well developed executive development programmes. But in Southern Italy, the Iberian peninsula outside Barcelona and Madrid, and in Greece progress in the development of management development has been seen.

Another major contrast is between large companies and small. The important role of large scale business in much of Europe has already been mentioned, but training in small business is much less extensive. Most EC countries have invested substantial sums in government aid to help small businesses start and to train their managers as the organisation grows. But in spite of these provisions and in spite of the growth of research and small business units in universities and business schools, management development in small companies remains problematical for very practical reasons, like the inability to spare managers for training and the cost of training as well as more attitudinal difficulties such as the belief among entrepreneurs that training is not relevant to the success of their business. The geographical imbalance of management educational facilities emphasises this problem because the poorer countries of Europe generally have a higher proportion of small businesses and fewer opportunities to train them.

The consequences of these difficulties could limit managerial mobility after 1992. There are different traditions of recruitment, training and development throughout Europe. The provision of training facilities varies widely. There are significantly different entry requirements to MBA programmes between centres, syllabuses vary in length and content. The nine business schools shown in the table below, taken from "Le Monde" (15th September, 1988), have some common features - age of entry for example does not vary widely. But the length of course is quite different and so is the length of professional experience. Language can also be a barrier. But differences are even more pronounced at national level. For example, those attending an MBA programme in the U.K. generally have an average age of 28. In France, traditionally the master's degree immediately follows the study of the first degree, whilst a manager coming from another country to West Germany would find virtually no provision for further study for a management qualification. Although management development activities have grown rapidly after a slow start, there remain many differences, anomalies and obstacles to the development of a European system which will ensure equal opportunities and common standards.

Table 1. International business schools in Europe

	IESE	IMEDE	IMI	INSEAD	ISA	LBS	MBS	RSM	SDA BOCCONI
Founded	1958	1957	1946	1959	1969	1966	1965	1970	1974
Status C = Chamber of Commerce P = Private U = University	U	P	P	P	C	U	U	U	U
Number of participants per programme	200	65	16	400	199	230	105	100	120
% National participants	66	13	7	30	80	62	70	65	85
% Other European nationals	13	40	41	46	10	13	20	15	10
% Participants from the rest of the world	21	47	32	24	10	25	10	20	5
Average age of participants	25.5	30	30	28	27	27	26.5	26	27
Professional experience demanded before entry	No	Yes	Yes	Yes	No	Yes	No	Yes	No
Cost of programme (in thousands of $)									
Europeans	9.0	20.0	23.5	16.5	11.0	15.0	14.05	12.0	12.5
Non-Europeans						22.0	21.275		
Length of programme (mo.)	21	11	10	10	16	21	21	18	16
Languages employed B = Bilingual D = Dutch E = English F = French I = Italian S = Spain	S B	E	E	E 80% F 20%	F 80% E 20%	E	E	E D	I 95% E 5 %
Average salary on leaving (in thousands of $)	36	72	74	60	50	50	35-90	25-30	-

IESE: Instituto de Estudios Superiores de la Empresa, Barcelona, Spain
IMEDE: Management Development Institute, Lausanne, Switzerland
IMI: International Management Institute, Geneva, Switzerland
ISA: Centre BEC-ISA, Chambre de Commerce de Paris, Jouy-en-Joas, France
LBS: London Business School, London, United Kingdom
MBS: Manchester Business School, Manchester, United Kingdom
RSM: Rotterdam School of Management, Erasmus University, Rotterdam, The Netherlands
SDA BOCCONI: Scuola di Direzione Aziendale, Università Luigi Bocconi, Milano, Italy

2. WHAT THE SURVEY REVEALED

All respondents agreed that the key factor influencing European business is vigorous competition. In the early 1980's this was felt most seriously in industries like steel, shipbuilding, heavy chemicals and traditional engineering as the newly emergent countries of the Pacific Rim - Japan, Korea, Taiwan, Malaysia, Singapore - challenged European companies on their own ground. The impact was enormous as one great company after another found its core business melting away. The resultant economic crisis and unemployment had an important impact on other industries like building materials, paper products, food and the complete range of consumer products. Since the early 1980's further shocks have been administered by the financial revolution, "deregulation" and the application of information technology not only to manufacturing but also to the service industries.

There is no company which has avoided the impact of these developments. Mature industries - paper and paper products, domestic appliances, glass and building materials, traditional engineering and car manufacturing are all well represented and interviewees all spoke of the impact of competition on their business as a continuing stimulus and challenge. Even those industries which were previously immune have been affected recently. An executive from the oil industry explained that the decline in the demand for oil is forcing oil companies downstream towards specialty chemicals. Deregulation and the information revolution are dramatically affecting banks as "invaders" attack their traditional areas of business, pointed out another respondent.

Companies see no let up in competitive pressure. In fact, with the arrival of the single market many of our interviewees see a further dramatic series of changes in European businesses. The sweeping away of trade barriers by 31st December 1992 will create a market of 320 million customers. The key moves to exploit this opportunity are already being made. There is considerable realignment in telecommunications. Mergers in France have increased considerably in 1988 and although some major battles have made the headlines, they have obscured other equally important moves. When the internal market becomes a reality, further rationalisation is likely. For example, it has been estimated that there is considerable over capacity in the telecommunications industry as the result of the desire of national PTT's to support a national telecommunications industry. Important moves are taking place in the automobile/aerospace sector and the opportunity for Europe to compete on equal terms with Japan and the United States will grow through the development of genuinely European companies and strategic alliances. But the United States and Japan also see the opportunities and threats of 1992 and are hardly likely to stand idly by.

Stability	------------>	Turbulence
National	------------>	International
Product focus	------------>	Market focus
Output	------------>	Productivity

Figure 1. Trends in the business environment

The Effects of the Changing Nature of Business

Mergers and acquisitions: The growing competition has had predictable effects. Some companies have attempted to make up for the low growth in mature industries by take-overs and acquisitions to help gain market share and some of them have been either victors or victims of this process.

Joint ventures and alliances: Companies have also attempted to strengthen their position by joining forces with others either to develop and implement a joint strategy towards particular markets or to combine forces to develop particular products. The managerial skills which are required to bring two former competitors with different cultures together to achieve common objectives are considerable. The task of organising effective project groups within a company is difficult enough, to achieve results between companies offers a difficult challenge.

Diversification: A third strategic approach has been to diversify to achieve a balanced portfolio into a range of distantly related (or unrelated) activities which it would be pointless to integrate but over which central financial control must be exercised. Several respondents represent companies who have experienced these processes. They agree that take-overs and acquisitions raise real issues for organisation and management development because of their impact on corporate culture, the organisational changes needed to derive the full benefits of new changes and the quality and quantity of management.

Innovation: A major response to increased competition has been very rapid product and market innovation. Many companies have almost completely changed their nature in a few years. From paper to electronics, for example, or from single-product to multi-product companies.

As far as products are concerned, the major change has been towards higher value added, greater complexity and more specialisation aimed at a particular market segment. Companies have attempted to define markets more closely and many have altered focus from a national to a European or from a European to a global view.

An overriding concern with the market is a characteristic shared by most companies, almost irrespective of their product. There has been a major shift from production- to market-centred management in the 1980s. Company after company identified the crucial importance of marketing orientation together with the importance of careful segmentation of the market. The cost of assembly of a computer amounts to only one-third of the marketing cost, to take just one example. Therefore, it is critically important that marketing is effective. Companies realise this and try to identify customer needs in carefully defined segments before beginning to introduce new products.

In successful marketing, price is the critical element. European companies are under pressure to deliver at very competitive prices. This has resulted in a ceaseless search for increased productivity in all its aspects and at every level of the organisation. This search has been considerably assisted by dramatic technological advances both in manufacturing and in the service industries. But the search has extended beyond the organisation itself. Many companies now subcontract work which they previously did themselves and which the subcontractors are required to produce "just in time". Thus new relationships are developing with suppliers which involve a greater degree of interdependence and imply a high degree of mutual understanding and trust. Suppliers' standards are vital. The efficiency and methods of distributors reflect on the company itself. The realisation that the boundary of the organisation is a membrane, not an insulation has led to the development of new organisational relationships backwards into production and forward into customer care.

Strategy	------------>	Structure
Centralisation	------------>	Decentralisation
Functions	------------>	Systems
"Hands"	------------>	Brains
Hierarchy	------------>	Networking
Soft culture	------------>	Hard culture
Individuals	------------>	Teams
Laisser faire	------------>	Social accountability

Figure 2. Organisational change - the trends

Organisational Consequences of Changes

The many environmental changes which are affecting our companies have been identified above. The organisational consequences are considerable.

Strategy --> Structure "Customers rule - o.k.?"

In today's world, the customer is king. The overriding aim expressed by many respondents is familiar - to get as close to the customers as possible and to meet their needs (at a level of price, quality and service which will give a competitive edge).

In most companies, very important - sometimes revolutionary - changes in organisational structure are taking place to enable this to happen. As strategies now have to change very rapidly, many companies are attempting to create structures flexible enough to meet market needs, rather than to continuously adapt their structure to rapid changes in strategy.

Centralisation --> Decentralisation   "The real issue is flexibility"

The most obvious manifestation of the change has been the rapid decentralisation of decision-making to local managers as close to the customer as possible. The managerial ramifications of this new focus are considerable:

- The balance of power changes. Head office is reduced to a core of very senior managers, controllers and specialists.
- Many staff functions are removed completely or decentralised to local companies. Intermediate levels disappear. The company becomes less of a hierarchy and more of a network.
- Represented visually, the structure ceases to look like the familiar pyramid in which all power is held at the centre and carefully devolved. Instead, it is more accurately represented as a galaxy in which the considerable power now rests with each "star" in the system.
- Local managers are held accountable for performance in ways which were not possible in centralised organisations. Business results become the criteria of success. Local managers become much more sharply focussed in their objectives.

Functions --> Systems

As a result of sharper business focus, functions are important only in as far as they serve the primary objective of the company. The company is organised as a total system devoted to winning business.

Hierarchy --> Horizontal networks

The danger in increasing local power is that an international corporation behaves like a series of small independent companies. There has been a development of networks to facilitate the transfer of knowledge, technology and standards from one part of the organisation to another.

But networking also extends beyond the corporation to dealers and distributors in the pursuit of customer care standards and to suppliers to ensure the effective implementation of "just in time" policies.

Hands --> Brains

When Henry Ford advertised for "hands" he was specifying exactly what he wanted - employees who would perform standardised, mindless tasks on assembly lines. Technology has changed all that. The modern business organisation relies much more on the co-ordinated activities of knowledge workers. They are well-educated, articulate and often in short supply. Their effective integration, motivation and commitment represents new challenges for management.

Individuals --> Teams

At one phase in the development of management training activities, it was felt that the development of "excellent" individuals would produce an "excellent" company. It was never true because all organisations need co-ordinated effort. In the new business organisations this has become even more important. The move from a functional to a system organisation means that the co-ordination of the work of varied specialists into one team becomes essential. The development of project groups to generate new products, customer care teams to service customers, total quality programmes to raise standards throughout the organisation, co-operation with suppliers, all presuppose a high degree of team work.

Soft culture --> Hard culture

All these trends have produced the need for corporate cultures which are results centred, tough, adaptive, able to communicate and demand high standards. This type of culture is becoming increasingly common and in the case of some companies represents a considerable change from the culture which preceded it. To achieve the change demands a thorough review of managerial practices, systems, leadership styles, value systems and philosophies.

Laisser faire --> Social accountability

Many companies have prided themselves on a strong sense of social responsibility but the pressure for accountability continues to rise. This is partly because many governments are suspicious of the activities of transnational companies and attempt to establish constraints on their activities. Additionally, an educated public is developing high sensitivity to ecological issues and exerts considerable pressure on business to behave responsibly.

Management Development in Flux

The work of Roger Harrison provides a useful framework for thinking about organisations. He distinguishes four basic types which can be identified by their differing concerns with integration and control. The following figure illustrates them.

Figure 3.
Organisation integration in relation to integration and control, I

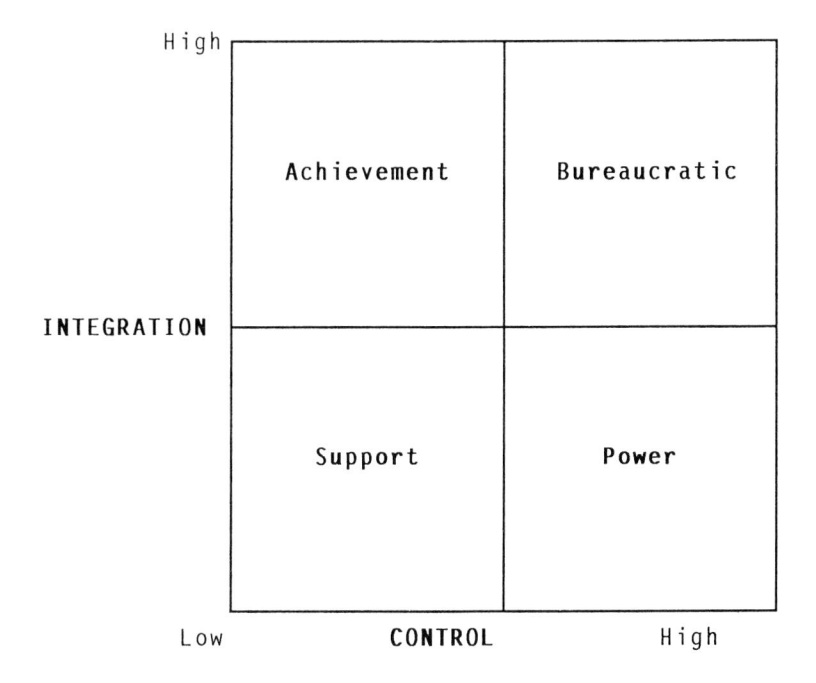

	Low CONTROL	High
High INTEGRATION	Achievement	Bureaucratic
	Support	Power

The features of each are quite distinctive:

- The bureaucratic role culture is hierarchical. Power is exercised through rules, systems and procedures. In these cultures people are motivated by rewards, punishments or systems.

- The achievement culture (often to be found in project teams and high-tech companies) is oriented to "making a difference" in the world. It provides opportunities for its members to use their talents in ways that are intrinsically satisfying and which advance a purpose or goal to which the individual is deeply committed. The achievement culture emphasises the "doing" values of action, autonomy, performance, innovation, building and shaping the environment. While working in such a culture can be deeply satisfying, it often makes high demands on its members' time and energy and can lead to "burn-out".

- The power culture is authoritarian and hierarchical and is driven by the exercise of personal power.

- The support culture motivates people through close, warm relationships. People learn to trust and care for one another and for the organisation and they expect the organisation to respond to their needs. As in the achievement culture, people are motivated "internally" rather than through external rewards and punishments. The support culture stresses values of co-operation, belonging, caring, responsiveness and receptivity. The weaknesses of this culture are that tough decisions about people may be postponed and that consensus may be over-valued so that the organisation cannot make timely decisions. It is this culture, however, that allows people to provide the more caring customer service.

The Implications for Organisational Type

The style and culture of each type of organisation obviously reflects on management development practices. Three approaches to management development are distinguished, based on the Harrison model - the fragmented, the formal and the focussed ("Management for the Future" sponsored by the Foundation for Management Education and Ashridge Management College, United Kingdom).

Figure 4.
Organisation integration in relation to integration and control, II

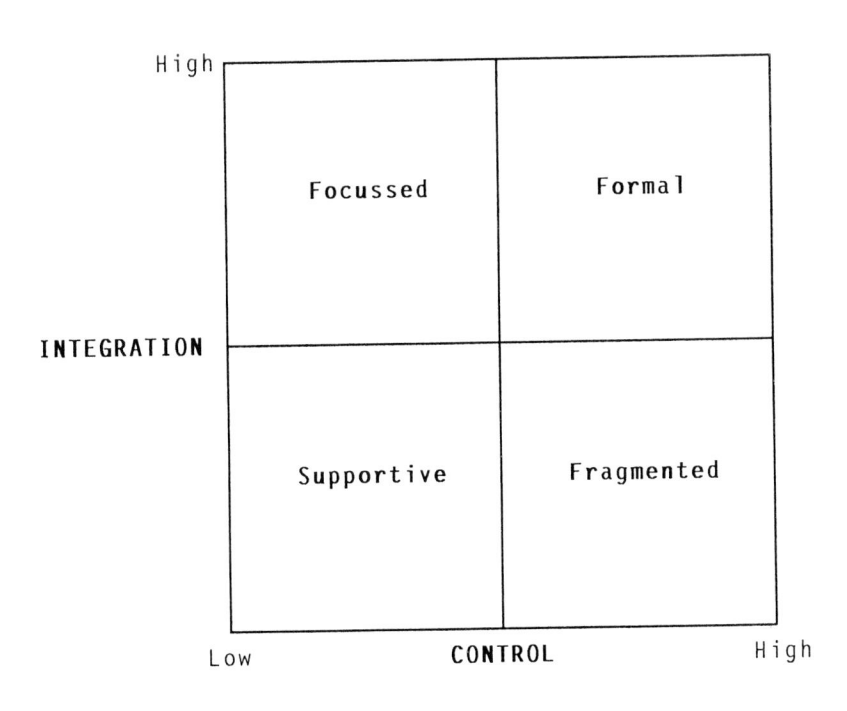

```
        High
              ┌─────────────────┬─────────────────┐
              │                 │                 │
              │    Focussed     │     Formal      │
              │                 │                 │
              │                 │                 │
INTEGRATION   ├─────────────────┼─────────────────┤
              │                 │                 │
              │    Supportive   │    Fragmented   │
              │                 │                 │
              │                 │                 │
              └─────────────────┴─────────────────┘
        Low          CONTROL              High
```

They could have gone on to identify a fourth - the supportive - in which the individual determines and satisfies his own development needs with the support of the organisation. They presumably found no examples of this type in their survey, but there are signs in a number of companies that such a style is beginning to emerge.

The "Management for the Future" survey makes the following distinctions between the three major approaches. They are set out below.

Fragmented:

- Training is not linked to organisational goals
- Training is perceived as a luxury or a waste of time

- Approach to training is non-systematic
- Training is directive
- Training is carried out by trainers
- Training takes place in the training department
- Emphasis on knowledge-based courses
- The focus is on training (a discontinuous process) rather than on development (a continuous process)

Formal:

- Training becomes linked to human resources needs
- Training becomes systematic by linking it to an appraisal system
- The emphasis is still on knowledge-based courses but the focus of the training course broadens, with greater emphasis on skill-based courses
- The link which is made between training and human resource needs, encourages organisations to adopt a more developmental approach. Broadly speaking, development in a formalised organisation means career development
- In terms of the emphasis that organisations place on training and development (apart from certain key areas), the value of the traditional training course is viewed with some scepticism, whereas development through career planning is highly regarded
- Training is carried out by trainers, but the range of skill demands placed on a trainer develops with the new breadth of courses offered
- Line managers become involved with training and development through their role as appraiser
- Pre- and post-course activities attempt to facilitate the transfer of off-the-job learning
- Training is carried out off-the-job, but through career development the value of on-the-job learning gains formal recognition
- There is more concern to link a programme of training to individual needs

Focussed:

- Training and development and continuous learning by individuals is perceived as a necessity for organisational survival in a rapidly changing business environment
- Training is regarded as a competitive weapon
- Learning is linked to organisational strategy and to individual goals
- The emphasis is on on-the-job development, so that learning becomes a totally continuous activity
- Specialist training courses are available across the knowledge/skill/value spectrum
- Self-selection for training courses
- Training is generally non-directive, unless knowledge-based
- New forms of training activity are utilised, e.g. open and distance learning packages, self-development programmes, etc.
- More concern to measure the effectiveness of training and development
- Main responsibility for training rests with line management
- Trainers adopt a wider role
- New emphasis on learning as a process
- Tolerance of some failure as part of the learning process- "droit d'erreur"

Supportive:

- Individuals accept responsibility for their own development
- Self-development plays a key role.
- Total support by the organisation.

There are very few companies whose training approaches may be described as fragmented. The great majority of companies fall into the **formal** category, but with a distinct trend towards **focussed** and **supportive** approaches. The following quotations from our respondents reflect focussed thinking.

- "The company is sceptical about training. Good managers are

> developed through practice. Formal training is not very important."

- "Line managers are responsible for employees' development. There are discussions at management group level and relevant organisations have to respond to the meeting."

In some companies the CEO will expect to spend several days a year actively participating in management development programmes.

- "Management development is closely connected to the general development of the company and changes in company structure. Top management is actively involved in the programme."

This important distinction between **formal** and **focussed** will be used in the following analysis.

3. MANAGERIAL SKILLS AND COMPETENCES

The survey produced a wide range of characteristics which companies look for in a manager. The list suffers all the usual difficulties. Some of the qualities are vague abstractions or mean different things to different people, or mean different things at different times. For example, the concept of leadership is quite different in the 80's from what it was in the 60's. Additionally the list offers little guidance in selection and development because the characteristics are difficult to measure or even identify in any useful way. If the more general abstractions are discarded, however, it is possible to identify a number of characteristics which can be conveniently grouped under three headings: predicting, persuading, and performing.

Predicting

Respondents identified a number of attributes which are concerned with the ability to predict possible futures. The most common is vision. It refers to the capacity "to dream a dream" to formulate some desireable future for the company. The dream, of course, must be capable of translation into reality. So, it must be dreamt by someone with an understanding of the product market relationships, who can identify key trends in the environment, who has the maturity to make sound decisions and who sees change as an opportunity. Such a person is normally tough and powerful, pro-active and flexible.

Persuading

But dreamers need other characteristics, those which help them to share their vision, communicate it to others and create the enthusiasm to achieve it. When our respondents used words like charisma, leadership, ability, capacity to communicate and motivate, organisational knowledge, networking skills, they were recognising the need for managers both to inspire others and to have presentational skills and organisational understanding to get their message across to the rest of the organisation and to the outside world.

Performing

One company, in its identification of the characteristics required in "high fliers" recognised that strategic vision must be associated with a sense of reality if it is to mean anything. Dreams without reality become fantasies. Reality without dreams becomes merely utilitarian. The successful manager must possess both, otherwise the dream will never be realised. Performing abilities include a thorough understanding of the key factors affecting excellent results, an understanding of basic economics and finance (to set clear goals and measure progress), the capacity for analysis, the ability to find new ways to goals, if the chosen path is blocked, the ability to manage and work in teams effectively and to use time effectively.

Managerial Skills in the 90's

Modern organisations are placing new demands on managers and require additional skills. No doubt every age has felt itself one of transition and change, but it must be particularly true of the present when large complex organisations must be managed in very turbulent environments.

The major environmental trends identified by respondents suggest that certain abilities and skills are becoming indispensable.

Market orientation: Every modern manager, indeed every member of staff, must be much more conscious than his predecessor of the market, the customer, quality and service if the business is to succeed. Similarly in a "knowledge" based "flatter" organisation, power must be exercised in quite subtle ways.

Persuasion and communication: The whole nature of the communication process becomes more subtle and more significant because intelligent, educated knowledge workers need convincing, not telling. This puts a high premium on persuasion, negotiation and presentation skills.

Team work: The role of the team grows increasingly important for two reasons. First, modern organisations are extremely complex. They draw on a wide range of specialist knowledge which need great skill to harness effectively into a total organisational effort. Secondly, in many modern organisations, temporary task forces and project teams are becoming quite commonplace. Selecting and training them, getting them motivated to achieve results is a difficult and demanding task. The modern manager must have the ability to not only build teams, but get them to work effectively and be an effective team worker himself.

The **organisation as a system:** Successful managerial results also depend on a thorough knowledge of the organisation as a system. At the more senior levels, managers must understand how to communicate, to exercise influence through the structure because in large-scale transnational organisations it is impossible for leaders to be everywhere. At lower levels, managers often need links with fellow specialists and peers across the organisation to learn from them, to benefit from their expertise and to help improve their results. To achieve the maximum benefits from the organisation, the manager needs to think of it as a system rather than as an assemblage of functions, and he needs knowledge of how it works both horizontally and vertically and as a network.

Cultural sensitivity: Many companies are not only large in themselves, they have also become culturally very complex, both in the obvious sense that they employ a wide range of nationalities, but less obviously through takeovers, mergers or strategic alliances with other organisations with a different history and at a quite different stage of development. Furthermore, the mother company is often faced with the challenge of developing an entirely new culture to tackle current business realities, and this was acknowledged by a number of respondents. One company, for example, said: "Our focus is on innovation, fast reaction and results." Another said, "We want to create a common language, a common way of thinking and treating people." In such conditions managers need to develop a sensitivity to cultural signals, an ability to both transmit and receive messages which are not obscured by cultural ambiguity. In this process a knowledge of languages is vital. Language is the key to cultural understanding. Although many companies now use English as a working language, it is not universal - certainly not at lower levels in the organisation. One company insists that its managers are fluent in at least one other language besides their mother tongue and others are giving it serious attention.

Results focus: Finally and obviously, managers in most companies are held firmly accountable for results. Operating in fast moving decentralised companies, managing demanding customers, a well-educated workforce, and a sometimes sceptical local community, it is not surprising that they feel themselves under increasing pressure and stress.

The real differences between the two types of companies lie not so much in their analysis of the skills required, but in what they do about it.

The formal companies tend to instill these skills in various categories of managers through structured programmes.

The focussed companies, whilst acknowledging the importance of these skills, take an "output" approach. They begin by analysing the business results expected of a manager, identify the behaviour required to achieve these results and attempt to identify the "key competencies" required for success. For example, the competencies required by a senior manager in a rapidly growing organisation are different from those required in one which is in slow decline. The problems of managing an acquired business contrast vividly with what one has needed earlier. To treat all these managers as a group of "senior managers" for development purposes and to send them on the same or similar programmes misses the point. The focussed company tries to undertake a much more detailed analysis and develop training solutions which are specific to the person.

All companies claim to be clear about the objectives of management development. The **formal companies** tend to have written statements which set out the goals very clearly and the survey revealed considerable agreement. They aim to:

- Provide skills to do the job
- Provide frames of reference to help decision making
- Develop new managers
- Create mobility for senior/high potential managers
- Support company efforts

The **focussed companies** emphasise the close connection between strategic change and management development and aim to:

- Create a competitive edge through excellent management
- Generate creative competence in the management team
- Encourage managers to take a pro-active stance in their work
- Improve corporate integration and innovation
- Create a new culture
- Help people to change

As one respondent put it dramatically, "If management development doesn't provide the high calibre people the business needs, we are dead!"

Apart from the stress on business development, the differences between the two are easily explained. **Formal organisations** usually have a well-defined culture. Part of the role of management development practices in this type of company is to introduce new managers to the culture and to get them to share its values. To this extent it is part of an important reinforcement process to help people to adopt the appropriate norms of organisational behaviour.

Focussed organisations want to change. To do this often entails breaking an old culture, sometimes violently, and embracing new values. In this process, management development plays a critical role in not only communicating, but helping to move the culture in a new direction. There are many examples in recent years of companies where the CEO (usually new to the company) has used massive training programmes to identify and implement key cultural changes vital to business success.

4. COMPARISON OF MANAGEMENT DEVELOPMENT PRACTICES

Common Elements

Most companies take management development very seriously, and <u>invest</u> heavily in it. Whilst it is not possible to quote budgets, the amount can be measured by the fact that some companies maintain their own staff college and have a large staff concerned purely with management development. Most companies use the major business schools (15-50 participants per year on average, but some have programmes tailored to their own needs, which increase numbers significantly).

There is also considerable <u>investment in time</u>. The survey reveals that on average managers spend between 5-10 days per year on training and development activities.

In many companies <u>responsibility for management</u> development rests within the CEO's office. As one respondent said, "It gives us a lot of clout." Senior managers are actively involved in programmes, as speakers, assessors, or project or programme leaders.

The Importance of Practical Training

Managers are primarily made through <u>practical experience</u>. Therefore, the more that the organisation is used positively as a source of learning, the stronger will be the development of its managers. Examples include:

- job rotation
- staff exchange between companies usually for bright young people

- projects and assignments within the company
- careful allocation of new jobs to test managerial ability
- secondment to university - to help start a development activity
- by a careful monitoring of performance in the current job

The **formal company** tends to rely on career planning in which a careful blend of a variety of types of experience is devised to produce the general manager. Development within the job relies on annual appraisals, redefinition of objectives and standards and appropriate counselling and training.

The **focussed company** uses the job much more actively as a learning opportunity. For example, managers are placed in exacting and difficult jobs as a deliberate measure of their potential. Quality improvement programmes are used consciously to create learning throughout the organisation.

Other companies expend considerable effort in ensuring that teams who must work together - on either a temporary or permanent basis - are initiated into their task with the help of consultants in team building and team working. The consultants help the team to establish values, standards and output criteria.

In all companies there is a strong <u>trend towards shorter, modular courses</u>, directly related to business objectives, with a strong emphasis on implementation of the learning experience.

It is recognised that managerial learning is a <u>lifelong activity</u>. Most leading companies have a range of programmes, some external, most internal, which managers must attend at critical points in their careers. But, as one executive said, "The lifelong learning process of continuing education is considered more important than the contents of any solitary, isolated experience; training and development cannot yield optimum results unless there is a balance between on-the-job and classroom learning; and attention must be given to the sharpening of skills (including especially human skills) and the removal of deficiencies."

Differences

There are, however, important differences both in philosophies and practices between formal and focussed companies. The key differences are:

Career development

Formal companies see change as evolutionary. They believe in a planned future, and careers are no exception. Lifelong employment is still a possibility in many European companies. These companies like to recruit young people and develop them over a total career by providing them with promotion and development opportunities.

Focussed companies have concluded for a number of reasons that lifelong careers are no longer so easy to guarantee. Mergers and acquisitions, changes of strategies, movement in the new markets, mean that planned development is difficult. Furthermore, as this type of company argues, fresh blood is useful. "10% of our managers are hired from outside. The strength in this practice is that you get alternative viewpoints, a fresh look at networking, away from earlier job concentration."

Focussed companies, therefore, rely less on formal appraisal systems and more on spotting high performance by the results managers get. The successful ones are then given more and more opportunities. This is career development through testing rather than planning. "These people should receive tasks that stretch them." Another respondent said, "We give the bright ones the most difficult jobs in the company. If they succeed, they are given more opportunities."

Management development and development managers

Focussed companies tend to be organised around decentralised profit centres which are very much the responsibility of the line managers and management development is their responsibility, too. It is the line manager who is the key person in determining development needs. He involves himself in it because he thinks it will produce practical results. He takes an active part in designing training which is often individualised and practice-based. Management development is part of his task.

In the **formal company**, the drive comes from management development staff, who learn of needs through the appraisal system, and discussion with line management.

Training programmes

Internal. Several companies have their own training centres, some quite lavishly housed and furnished with the provision of the latest educational technology. Practice varies in these centres, but generally programmes are organised by "programme directors" who design and arrange courses which are staffed by a mixture of line managers and consultants - often professors of business schools. A structure of courses is typical of the majority of both formal and focussed companies.

The differences between the formal and focussed lies in the methodology rather than in the structure of programmes. In the formal companies, participants become eligible for programmes at a certain stage in their career and automatically go through them. The programmes tend to be structured, knowledge- and classroom-based, reliant on traditional methods of instruction.

In the **focussed companies** the selection of participants is more related to specific needs. Programmes tend to be shorter and the learning methods less traditional. For example, they include workshops on strategy rather than classical seminars. "Shorter training periods, 2-3 days, flexibility, rapid transfer of new knowledge into practice." In some cases, the methods have changed radically. One company has completely re-oriented its business development programmes to focus on current problems in the business. Participants spend a high proportion of the time working on a problem to which they must find a solution. The course, which involves 25 participants directly, in fact involves 60 in the learning process including the senior line managers, who are responsible for briefing the group and evaluating the results and those who are actually managing the process under examination. So far this programme has saved the company 3,000,000 ECU's with its innovative solutions.

A similar approach is used in another company when the entire second week of the international management programme is devoted to real projects. A typical example is the investigation of a new distribution system. The case was set by the managing director of a subsidiary. His staff were actively involved in briefing for the project and providing data, and visits were made to a variety of distributors and other subsidiaries. Specialists were consulted, other companies' practices reviewed, and literature searches made. The solution was proposed to the managing director after six days of hard work. He was sufficiently impressed to ask the group to continue their work after the end of the programme and their proposals were eventually incorporated into his annual plan.

These examples demonstrate that this type of action-centred learning is very sophisticated in its approach. Those involved in proposals and briefing must understand management thinking and learning methods to be able to choose and prepare projects wisely. Groups need careful guidance, which presupposes sound formal knowledge. Otherwise the project method can be very expensive and wasteful.

5. COMPANY-WIDE ACTION PROGRAMMES

The most dramatic demonstration of the relationship between management development and the improvement of business effectiveness is shown in the training activities - often involving thousands of staff - which have been launched in a number of companies to change attitudes to total quality and service. The standards are set at corporate level and subsidiaries are given support. But it is the local managers and their teams - the key personnel - who attempt to re-orient attitudes and practices to quality and customers in order to provide the company with a useful competitive edge. In **formal companies** these activities are thought to lie within the scope of the management development department. In **focussed companies** they are regarded as a core management activity.

External: The Consortium Programme

Some companies use the "consortium" programme. This represents an attempt to bring together a group of usually senior managers to focus on issues which several companies might have in common, and can be shared without problems of commercial secrecy, for example, environmental change. Their development is sometimes motivated by frustration with external institutions and a feeling that the companies can do better for themselves. In practice, many companies find these courses a mixed blessing. It is difficult to choose the right partners, to get the right levels of participants together, or to pick a subject which can be generally shared. But one company mentioned that at a very senior level it feels a pressing need to create a forum with other companies where mangers can learn from each other's experience - for example in handling mergers and alliances. The organisation of such courses demands considerable skill.

Business Schools

Most major companies use business schools for purposes which include:

- widening experience through mixing with managers from other companies
- courses "tailored" specifically to the needs of a particular company
- business school professors involved in "in-company" programmes

Benefits

The following benefits emerged as the most obvious:

- an opportunity to mix with managers from other organisations: "Business schools mainly serve for networking, so that you can compare yourself with others"
- a facility or service which cannot be offered internally
- the opportunity to meet and learn from first-class teachers
- the opportunity to develop new networks and contacts

Value

The overwhelming attitude to the school is positive and supportive. Many of those who took part in the survey would agree with an article in "Fortune" (May 23, 1988): "Europe's best schools offer a pedagogic product that their bigger, older US rivals do not. While students and courses at Harvard or Wharton are largely American, European schools have an overwhelmingly international student body and point of view. Students study, socialise, and negotiate with classmates from Spain, India, Japan and as many as 20 other countries - all in English. From that rich cultural mosaic come managers who understand how foreigners think and global markets work."

The companies in the survey would endorse this comment, not only in relation to the schools mentioned in the article, but to many excellent national schools. Concerns exist about the MBA programmes, learning methodologies and the supply and quality of staff.

6. THE INTERNATIONAL MANAGEMENT DIMENSION

Most companies express a great deal of interest in internationalisation. For all of them, it has become a major preoccupation and they are spending substantial time and money to make sure that they have the managers equipped to operate on a European, if not global scale.

Many do considerable business in other countries and have done for many years but remain essentially national in their orientation. One respondent defined a truly international company (apart from the usual criteria) as one in which the top management is multinational - especially the headquarters team, in which selection for managerial jobs is based simply on talent, with as many ideas for development coming from outside the home country as from within.

In a very few cases, companies have moved their headquarters from the mother country. This has happened for a variety of reasons. Not only to develop an international culture - but it has certainly helped to do so. Some companies set up international training facilities away from the home country - and hold programmes in several cultures.

The issue poses many problems, some outside the scope of this survey. Examples include reward systems, how to reintegrate executives into the system when they return to home base, or how far the national characteristics are a help or a handicap. Sometimes, it is a positive advantage to stress national characteristics if this helps sales - for example **Scandinavian or Italian** design is a strong selling point. The export of a national culture can, however, cause difficulties with the workforce.

From a management development point of view, companies find it important to define exactly what the term international management means. One company makes the following distinctions:

> **Expatriate managers** who live and work in another country. These represent a tiny fraction of the total managerial workforce. In a particular country typically only the chief executive and two or three other senior executives might be expatriates. Even these numbers are likely to be reduced as countries become sensitive to the needs of their own nationals.

Companies naturally give considerable attention to this group who are the key links with the mother organisation. Development practices include:

- Attendance at international programmes arranged by the handful of international business schools in Europe and the United States
- detailed briefing on the new post and the new country at corporate headquarters
- attendance at international briefing centres or courses by specialists in cultural differences (often attended by the spouse, too) - of which very few exist
- pre-visits to the company and introduction of senior staff and customers
- support, especially in the early stages from visiting executives and specialists
- early identification of the next career move
- language training if appropriate

Visiting specialists, e.g. accountants, systems experts, human resource managers, etc., who provide advice and help. They are short-term visitors to a variety of countries. Many companies are careful to choose them with particular attention to their ability to adapt to other cultures and their curiosity about different places and systems. Companies often provide them with the opportunity to attend selected international programmes. They also try to create the opportunity to develop long-term relationships by linking them with particular countries and companies, rather than using them as general "firemen".

Deskbound managers and other staff who have international connections and form an important link between subsidiaries and head office. Their training needs include a clear understanding of the sensitivities involved in the head office/subsidiary and nation/nation relationships. The ability to handle these relationships positively is regarded in some companies as a key performance requirement. They must have at least some understanding of the country and company they deal with. A number of companies arrange special training for those in this category. It includes detailed briefing on the country and company as well as an opportunity to meet the key executives with whom they deal.

English is the formal language of communication in many companies, and is becoming accepted as the international language. But even where English is the general means of communication, subsidiaries normally use the language of their country informally and at the shop-floor level. Expatriate managers or the visiting consultants who are unfamiliar with the language suffer a distinct handicap. Some companies believe that those who travel widely should be given the opportunity to learn at least one additional major European language. For cultural understanding, basic language competence is essential anyhow.

7. PINPOINTING MANAGEMENT POTENTIAL

Within the ERT group of companies, much attention is given to the identification of "high fliers". Each company has a core of potentially senior managers whose progress is carefully monitored. The means by which they are identified vary.

Formal companies tend to operate detailed personnel planning systems. These are used to identify potential high fliers and to follow them throughout their career. One purpose is to provide a filter and in the process make potential top managers visible. The following example is typical of how such systems work.

> "We have a 'cadre' of about 200 managers. They are employed by the group rather than by any individual division or subsidiary. It is from this group that we will select our leaders for the future. They are corporate staff and we look after all aspects of their career. In general, they are usually 30 years old or more."

Focussed companies prefer to avoid complex appraisal systems and monitor business units carefully to spot those who get good results. They are often given exacting assignments to measure their potential.

> "Visibility is important. It depends on developing a good track record."

Whatever the method used to identify potential managers, there is agreement among companies on the need to expose them to a variety of managerial experiences and to help them to develop the appropriate knowledge and skill.

The range and type of experience differs from one company to another, but some of the following aspects are commonly evaluated:

Learning to run a whole business. Every potential senior manager must at some point learn to run a whole business. This calls for quite different skills from those which have yielded success in the past. The importance of this kind of experience early in a potential leader's career is stressed in a number of ways. Young managers are placed at an early stage in their careers in small business units where they learn to develop general management rather than functional skills.

> "In our group a branch manager is the first position with full profit responsibility. Those that perform well have the opportunity to move on; those that do not are moved sideways."

International experience. In many companies, senior managers must have the ability to operate internationally. The ability to become a successful leader in the home country is also enhanced by international experience because of a greater understanding of the group as a whole.

> "We must have people with international experience to run our global business."

> "Managers who work abroad have to question deeply almost every concept they have about management. As a result, they have to rethink their ideas. This makes them much more effective when they return home."

Learning to develop subordinates - givers and takers. Top managers usually play a very direct role in developing their successors. In most people's view, the ability to do this is a prerequisite for anyone wishing to enter the top team.

> "A key element is the development of people within the business. Everyone who expects to join our top team must have proved that he can develop at least three people capable of replacing him in his previous job."

In two companies in the survey the development of subordinates is written into task objectives. "Givers", those who have the capacity to develop subordinates, are soon distinguished from "takers", those who centre their attention purely on the immediate task.

Learning to think strategically. Many people stress the need for an aspiring business leader to develop his ability to think strategically, and to be able to translate this into concrete results. There were a number of approaches in practice.

> "We want our future leaders not only to be analytical but also implementors - they have got to be able to translate ideas into practice. To help them we give them experience in headquarter departments, but they also must take on difficult line jobs."

Managing through the structure. Some people enter a company with a number of basic skills and aptitudes which make them more likely to succeed than others. However, the learning process inside the company is critical. The ability to work as part of a management team is certainly important, as is the awareness of the need to develop and deploy personal power through the operating structure.

> "The more senior the manager, the more he must be a 'team' person. The 'one-man band' cannot run an international company."

> "Our best managers are successful networkers. They know how to get critical information into and out of the system."

Ability to transfer managerial competence. Some companies are multi-business enterprises. Leadership in such groups is extremely sophisticated and complex because managers must be able to generalise their experience developed in one business and apply it to others where the criteria for success may be quite different.

> "Our managers must be able to take their experience with them and apply it in totally different circumstances."

Planned formal programmes. Most companies create the opportunity for high potential managers to attend a series of internal programmes at various stages of their development. At the more senior levels, they attend carefully selected business school programmes where the manager will meet peers from other companies and high-quality professors.

Planned action programmes. Increasingly, the managers are also involved as leaders, tutors and participants in the type of action-learning programmes centred on business results, especially in focussed companies.

Teaching in business schools. Some companies encourage their managers to become visiting teachers. They feel that it helps develop self-confidence, keep managers up-to-date and acts as a stimulus to thinking about management.

Success on the job - key criterion. But most respondents stressed that, above all, it is the results achieved which make a business leader.

> "In the end we have to judge by results."

In response to this organisational re-orientation, management development is changing dramatically to become more business-driven, action-led and results-oriented. Approaches to learning are becoming more varied. The focus is switching from the classroom to the business. New technologies are being harnessed to help the learning process. The traditional boundaries between formal education and practical training and development are becoming less distinct. Management development is seen as a key element in the winning of a competitive edge. But to really capitalise on these advances certain initiatives must be taken.

Europe needs competent and professional managers at every level. Training an elite is a necessary but not sufficient precondition for business success. There is a particular need to ensure that small and medium-sized companies, who supply the key components to large businesses and distribute their products, are professionally managed.

Unfortunately, because of lack of opportunity, time, and cost problems, many managers in these organisations receive little or no training. Nor do all large companies provide the training necessary to produce professional managers for themselves. As the quality of management becomes a key factor in developing a competitive edge, it is essential that the opportunity for management training and development be widely extended. This will require substantial expansion of the existing system and the employment of new technologies.

Poor feedback systems pose the danger that business schools will not find it easy to keep up with evolving company demands. Particular concerns were expressed by respondents in the survey concerning:

- the ability of national schools to meet the need for the "Europeanisation" of management

- the willingness to adapt to or to develop new learning technologies, e.g. action-learning, the application of new technologies to learning, etc.

- the supply of staff, their quality and ability to keep up-to-date

- the flexibility to adapt to new patterns of learning, e.g. modular programmes and part-time courses.

8. COPING WITH DEMAND THROUGH FLEXIBILITY

To cope with this demand the existing system must become more flexible. It is **recommended** that:

- more flexible modular and part-time qualification programmes be developed to allow a wide population access to management education

- qualification programmes are developed in conjunction with companies to meet their specific needs and/or to ensure that certain in-company courses are accepted as creditworthy in qualification programmes

- a credit accumulation and transfer system be developed in the European Economic Space

- business schools should agree not only on the harmonisation of standards for qualifications throughout Europe but should aim to raise them.

Companies should release managers for a minimum of five days a year to enable them to keep up-to-date. New learning systems should be employed more widely and more extensive use should be made of action-learning approaches already employed in focussed companies.

The survey has stressed the importance of language facility. Action is necessary at several levels.

Recommendations:

- managers should master two languages in addition to their own

- language education should begin at an early age in schools

- more joint management/language courses should be developed at the under-graduate level

- the opportunity to develop languages at the MBA level should be encouraged

- the facility to learn languages in the company through distance learning systems or through conventional means should be provided

- multi-language support material should be developed

It is **recommended** that regional organisations should help define the emerging needs for management development more precisely, as a preliminary to further initiatives at a regional and national level.

- Regional organisations are **recommended** to develop programmes to encourage the exchange of staff and students between European centres and co-operation concerning qualification and post-experience programmes. Research into management should also be encouraged across frontiers.

- Business schools are **recommended** to seek European partners to develop joint programmes at under-graduate, graduate and post-experience levels as quickly as possible.

There is still a wide misunderstanding of the role of business in society. To correct this, action needs to be taken.

- In schools, a number of enterprising initiatives have already been taken in this area - the use of competitive simulations, young entrepreneur schemes, etc. - but much more effort must be made to help young people understand the role of business.

- Civil servants and businessmen often find difficulties of mutual understanding. The ability and encouragement to move from a career in government to one in business should be encouraged. This is already done with success in France and Finland, for example, and more initiatives should be encouraged by business.

9. SUPPLY OF TEACHERS

There is a desperate shortage of management teachers in all community countries. Recent research (1988) by the University of Lancaster based on the evidence of more than 50 management education institutions in Europe concludes:

- There will be considerable growth in management education/development at degree and post-experience levels over the next five years. This planned growth is, however, likely to lead to major problems, particularly in the recruitment of new faculty and in helping existing faculty adjust to new market opportunities

- 70% increase in activity overall with newer institutions predicting faster growth (range 10% to 370% growth)

- for different areas of activity the approximate figures are: student numbers (+ 30%), executive education (+ 70%), research and consultancy (+ 150%)

- staff numbers are planned to rise by about 35%.

A number of problems are evident in relation to the recruitment of managers. It is, and will be difficult to recruit new faculty at the rate required. Output of doctoral programmes is insufficient to provide the staff required and it is getting very hard to attract faculty from industry due to salary differentials.

Recommendations:

- Much more radical thinking is needed to deal with the teacher shortage. The reliance on Ph.D.'s as the only source of supply will lead to a worsening of the current situation. It is **recommended** that a one-year course is introduced, which will allow business managers who wish to do so to move into management teaching. It is also recommended that much more extensive use is made of practising managers and consultants on a part-time basis.

- A radical approach is also needed to salary systems. The reward gap between industry and business schools must be reduced to attract talented staff. This will require considerable funding.

- Privately endowed management institutions have been very successful in several Community countries because of their greater flexibility. It is **recommended** that more university business schools should be encouraged to set up on an independent basis.

Much more attention should be given to in-service training. Currently only one programme exists at the European level. This is pitifully inadequate. Young staff need help to develop learning methodologies; more mature staff need help to keep up-to-date. Faculty development practices and the resources devoted to them are inadequate and should be substantially increased.

10. OPEN LEARNING SYSTEMS

An increasingly complex society will make demands on education and training on a lifelong basis. It is estimated that by the year 2000 adult workers will require retraining four times in their working lives. A wider variety of delivery systems must be utilised to allow access to learning to all who need it and to ensure that scarce teaching resources are effectively used.

Open learning systems denote flexible arrangements offering a choice of how, when and where to learn. They are becoming readily available, more versatile and more necessary. Their effectiveness in the teaching of basic management disciplines has already been demonstrated through the Henley Distance Learning MBA, which is in use not only in the U.K. but also in other European countries.

A number of companies are already exploiting the fact that many staff work on personal computers and video recorders to make available a wide range of cassettes and simulation exercises to encourage self-learning. Some business schools are also developing the means which enable participants to identify their own learning needs and to satisfy them in self-learning centres. But there is substantial room for experimentation and co-operation to fulfil the potential of these new opportunities both in business and in educational institutions.

It is **recommended** that:

- Companies monitor developments, encourage the exchange of information, and experiment in the application of new methods. Co-operation with educational institutions is also recommended to encourage joint development.

On a wider scale, there are signs that Europe is being outpaced by the United States, which is already involved in 80 major nationwide projects based on open systems learning, and by Japan.

It is further **recommended** that:

- The development of the Euro-PACE programme be carefully monitored to judge how it could be developed and applied to management training and development.

Attitudes to business schools are generally positive and constructive. This is particularly true in relation to national schools, some of which are rated very highly. European schools now are often preferred to their American counterparts for many programmes - a situation which would not have been conceivable a few years ago. But not surprisingly, there are criticisms.

The MBA Programme

The most serious criticism focusses on international full-time MBA programmes. Almost without exception companies found the graduates arrogant: "They expect to be running the business in three years," or expensive: "To employ an MBA would entirely upset our salary structure." The Business Graduates Association for example finds that MBA graduates with work experience can expect to increase their salary by 60% when they rejoin the workforce, in addition to which they ill equipped to deal with operational problems.

Recommendations:

There are a number of ways of dealing with this issue.

- As the companies participating in the survey employ very few MBA's, they should identify those schools which are capable of designing a manufacturing- or technologically-based MBA of high-quality and co-operate with them to produce it and support them when they have done so. This will allow the existing schools to continue to produce MBA graduates of high quality for finance, consultancy and the strategic planning departments of large multinationals.

- Schools should modify their MBA programmes to stress the implementation of strategy as well as strategy formulation. Practical projects should be used more extensively to reinforce the importance of action as well as concepts.

- Whilst the creation of more opportunities to study management is welcome, the use of the term MBA to cover a very wide variety of programmes, which vary in content, time and depth, means that the worth of a qualification is becoming very difficult to determine. Schools are urged to find a means of regulating the current qualifications system to enable potential clients to determine with some confidence which form of study and level of qualification suits them best.

11. DEVELOPMENT OF A EUROPEAN APPROACH

Many companies are worried that excellent national schools have not yet developed into excellent European schools and it is an urgent requirement that they should do so.

It is **recommended** that companies support:

- Partnerships between schools across frontiers. With their combined faculties, they can offer international courses designed for specific companies

- The creation of opportunities for faculty and corporate staff to work together on research in conjunction with other companies

- The involvement of corporate staff to teach in business schools in other countries. Some companies expect young high-potential managers to become visiting professors - a development of mutual benefit.

- The willingness to become a source of project work and case material for participants in programmes from other countries.

Partnership

The ultimate aim must be to produce a genuine partnership between schools and businesses. A useful model for management development is the clinical one. Doctors are trained not only in theory but also in its application in practice. A doctor is not qualified until he has "walked the wards". The true test of a manager is in what he achieves in practice. This means that the successful manager can only be produced if business and business schools work together. There are already many examples of this co-operation. It can be fostered by:

- the encouragement of young executives to teach in business schools on a regular basis

- creating the opportunity for school staff to work in the business either on research projects, the preparation of teaching material, or for longer periods to update their practical knowledge

- the development of means to allow companies to communicate their needs effectively by becoming active members of a consortium associated with a business school

- the development of joint activities in which the boundaries between school and business begin to blur

A closer collaborative effort is called for. Innovative approaches to teaching and learning, which demand active co-operation between the parties, are essential to provide the managers who will lead successful European business in the twenty-first century. Not only do business schools need to rethink their strategies, organisation and cultural orientation - as European industry has done so vigorously in the last few years - but they need the help of European business to fund major new investments in equipment and staff so that a joint development effort can be created.

It is important both for Europe and companies themselves to help improve the practice of management in the medium and smaller enterprises, which provide many of the key components for large manufacturing companies or are key factors in the distribution system.

In the same way that companies insist on quality in terms of products and services received from their suppliers, they could also insist on certain standards of management training and development. It is **recommended** that they should help suppliers by making available their own management development facilities. Undoubtedly, this would act as a powerful incentive to many medium and small companies which it has been found very difficult to influence in other ways, particularly as many large companies are in a position to influence a considerable number of smaller firms. Some companies already train distributors. The need to train suppliers is equally important given the development of sub-contracting and the need to maintain high-quality standards.

These ideas have the additional merit that corporate training becomes a profit centre and its performance can be measured by results.

12. THE EUROPEAN MANAGEMENT MODEL

In the developments taking place it is possible to see an emergent European model of management development. It builds on the cultural diversity of Europe, which capitalises on the ability of European managers to move across frontiers with a sensitivity to a variety of cultural norms and an ability to recognise the opportunities offered by diversity rather than the problems.

It maintains a very pragmatic approach to learning opportunities. It uses the business itself as a source of learning, which helps to integrate theory and practice. It flourishes as a genuine partnership between business schools and business itself.

Much of this development is still at an embryonic stage. Practice and standards vary from one country to another and especially between companies, but not only between large and small ones. Much remains to be done to raise the standards of management in Europe as a whole to a level where business can regard itself as totally capable of competing globally. Nevertheless, the signs are encouraging. The implementation of these recommendations will make a real contribution to further progress.

Photo Courtesy Volvo

PART VI
LIFELONG LEARNING AND ADULT EDUCATION

L.M. Jarenko and M. Otala

1. FROM RESTRUCTURING INDUSTRY TO RESTRUCTURING WORK

Technological development is changing the structure of industry and business. The life-span of products is constantly shortening. In certain sectors of electronics, for example, it is only a couple of years. Knowledge and competence become outdated equally fast. For the people who design, manufacture and market products, this means continuous renewal and development of their individual skills.

Work procedures and work itself are facing restructuring, too. The contents and structure of jobs are changing. Ever higher competence is expected in all occupations. For instance, instead of merely handling money, bank employees are more and more often experts on more complex financial matters as well. They must master the new instruments of information technology. More and more individuals are being confronted with the stark reality that their education, completed decades ago, no longer gives them the competence they need; indeed, the very occupation for which that education prepared them is receding below the horizon of history.

The role of company resources has changed as well. Whereas production facilities and buildings used to be regarded as investments and labour as a cost, the way in which their roles are often seen today is the reverse. Since manufacturing technology is integrated into products, it - and possible even an entire factory - becomes obsolescent along with it. The only factor that remains unchanged is the personnel, whose tenure is also supported by legislation. **Thus personnel is a long-term investment** that needs constant maintenance.

Table 1. Changing world in accounting

Resource	Past	Future
Materials	cost	cost
Labour	cost	investment
Machinery	investment	cost
Buildings	investment	(cost)
Market share	-	investment

2. THE NEW EMPLOYEE AND NEW VALUES

In an agricultural society people usually had only one occupation as long as they lived. With the advent of industry, many people had several jobs in the course of their lifetime. The modern information society offers us many more opportunities, but increasingly limits the duration of careers. Having to change from one job to another and even to a new occupation means that people must have the opportunity to supplement and upgrade their education, and possibly to undergo retraining.

With the rising standard of living, **the perception of and esteem accorded work has changed.** It is no longer done only to earn money, but is increasingly seen as a means of finding new contents in one's life and a way of fulfilling oneself. Young well-educated people, in particular, have brought **new values** to working life. They expect a job to give new challenges and **a chance for self-development.** Motivation is not achieved solely through the allurements of good pay or a leading position in the organisation. A variety of tasks and new challenges are just as enticing. Many careers in a lifetime are thus also something that an employee actually wants, and not just a necessity dictated by the restructuring of work.

3. HOW IS INDUSTRY RESPONDING TO THE CHANGES?

Earlier, in times of continuous growth, industry coped with the demands of technological development by employing young, newly-graduated people with up-to-date knowledge and skills. But at the same time as structural adjustment brought about unemployment, competent young people began to be a sought-after resource, and many new industries began suffering outright labour shortages.

The OECD has estimated that the number of young people aged 16-24 entering working life will decrease by close to 10 per cent by 1995. Consequently it is estimated that the average age of the working population will increase by one year every two years. By the year 2000 we will have a considerable manpower shortage in Europe. Companies will no longer be able to obtain infusions of new and up-to-date knowledge by recruiting young graduates. Nor will they be able to afford the luxury of promoting competent professionals to management positions (many of them will have to be moved laterally to fill urgent needs) or of transfering persons with outdated skills to administrative posts - or declaring them redundant.

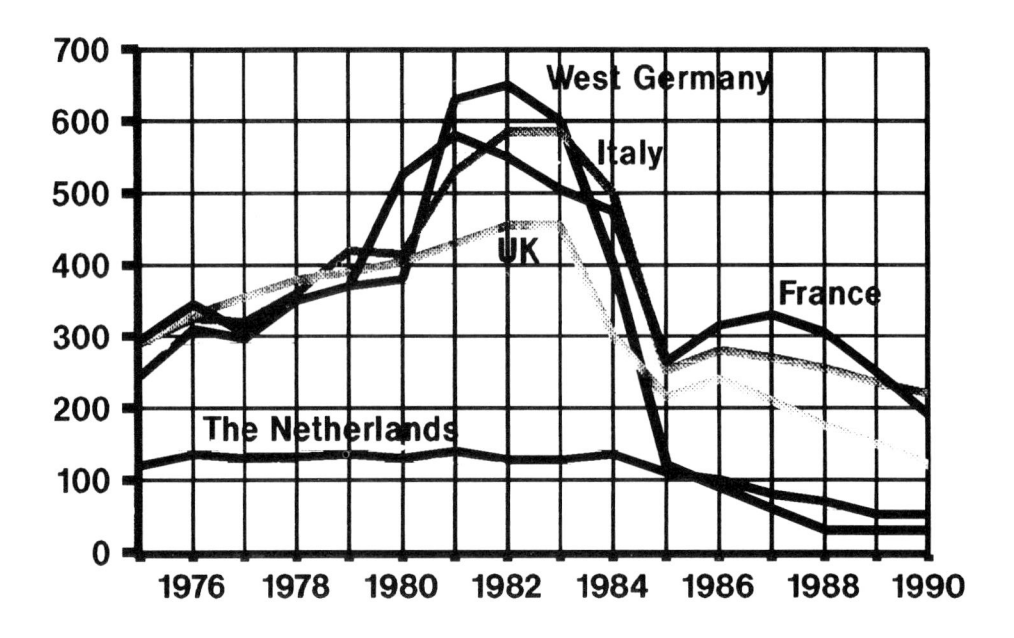

Figure 1. Number of 15-year-olds entering the labour force minus 65-year-olds leaving it

Competitiveness will have to be ensured by keeping competence updated. This will create a considerable need for adult education and training.

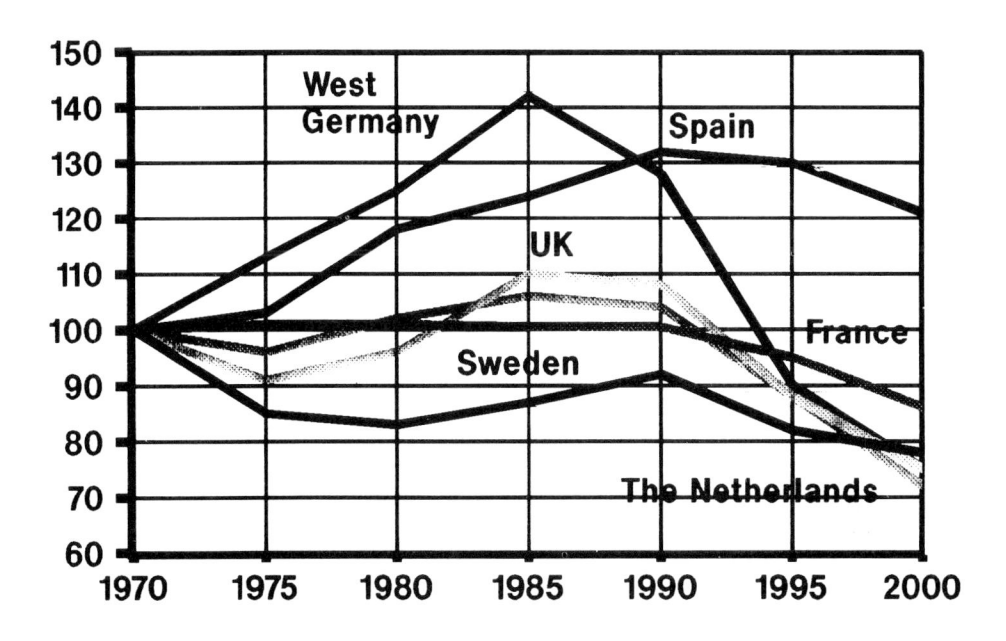

Figure 2. Student boom and slump - population aged 20-24

4. ADULT EDUCATION - THE NECESSITY BORN OF RESTRUCTURING

The constant need for continuous and re-education in Europe relates to the entire working-age population: 268.5 million people. The European unemployment rate averages 9.8 per cent, which alone means 20 million jobless. The immediate need for retraining is already enormous, and with continuous restructuring will continue to increase. The need for supplementary and continuous education and training of employed people will also increase. Constant learning is now needed most in the new high-tech industries, but technological development is making it necessary in most other fields as well.

5. OBSTACLES TO PROGRESS IN ADULT EDUCATION

European education has not yet responded to the new challenges posed by restructuring of industry and work and demographic changes. Attitudes in schools and among students, as well as in the labour market, are obstacles. The rigidity of education systems is reflected in these attitudes. Many myths shackle the development of education:

> **Life is still perceived as being divided into stages:** study, using what we have learned, and old age. Study is a necessary evil, after which we can enjoy life. **Study and work are seen as separate and different paths of life.** Among other things this implies that when studying one should not have a job, and when working one should not study. An employee pursuing continuing studies is not "efficient and reliable". All learning is expected to end at the age of retirement, when a person is "put out to grass".
>
> Constant changing of jobs involves constant learning of new things. **Education is not a once-and-for-all event** but a continuous process. Life is constant learning. Consequently, lifelong learning should be made the concept of competence for Europe. Studying must constitute a part of work and life. At their best they coincide: work offers the best opportunity for study. Study leave for one or two years is not needed in this case. Instead, studies are pursued alongside work for shorter periods.
>
> In general, education has been discussed as **a subject concerning only young people.** Schools and universities are for young full-time students only. By thirty, at the latest, they are expected to have graduated. That, however, is just the time when a new eagerness to study is usually awakened, together with the realisation that the knowledge acquired through basic education will carry them no further. 40-year-olds, whose professional competence is outdated, have the greatest need for re-education.

The school is an institution where knowledge is imagined to flow magically into the students' brains. The teacher is an authority whose erudition is supreme. To learn you have to go to school and to the teacher. This inevitably implies that pursuing studies is a full-time job that does not integrate into life outside. **Work, however, is the best education and teacher.** New methods to provide instruction for working adults should be developed. It is easier to move a teacher and tools of learning than a great number of students. Learning is at its best when it is part of work and daily life.

6. ADULT EDUCATION AND TRAINING LACK MODELS

Education and training intended for adults have mainly consisted of short-term courses. The actual competence of the participants is not likely to increase during separate ad-hoc courses. **An open university** is one of the first opportunities for more target-oriented long-term studies. However, open universities have been rather slow to get underway in many countries, as sufficient resources have not been reserved. In the U.K. and the Netherlands, where open universities have existed longer than elsewhere and where their scope is broadest, interest in studies intended to lead to a degree is greatest among those students who are over 30, i.e. past the normal studying age.

Table 2. Distance university enrolments and characteristics of degree-seeking students: 1984[1]

	Open University UK	UNED Spain	Distance University West Germany	Open University Netherlands	Sweden
Number of degree students in distance universities, %	67,800	44,944	13,185	21,694	10,000
Distance degree students as a proportion of all degree students, %	8	8	1	7	5
Age under 25, %	4.6	23	16	18.7	NA
25-30, %	17.9	33 (31-38)	45 (25-31)	25.1	NA
31 and over, %	77.5	44	39 (32+)	56.2	NA
Employment status: Employed, %	80.2[2]	77	87	68	NA

(1) Or nearest year
(2) 5.1 per cent of total described as housewives with part-time work up to 20 hours per week

Source: CERI (1985)

The open university is an appropriate step towards organising adult education, and is an alternative to be recommended in various European countries. Open universities in different countries could co-operate by recognising each others' courses, thus enabling students to include instruction given at two or more universities in their own education programmes.

7. STILL LARGELY A COMPANY RESPONSIBILITY

Responsibility for educating and training the working population is increasingly being assumed by companies. Corporate educational investments have increased constantly as industry becomes more technology intensive. Many major European companies spend between 1 and 6½ per cent of wages and salaries on education and training. High-tech companies are among the biggest spenders. However, overseas competitors often invest much more in competence. The total spent by one major American high-tech company on training and education represents the same proportion of its turnover as European companies' corresponding figure represents in their wage bill, i.e. about 1 per cent. In the USA, industry's investment in education already exceeds the figure spent on education provided by all universities and colleges.

8. OPEN LEARNING - A KEY TO ADULT EDUCATION

Learning takes place everywhere, as does studying. **Education is an attitude** and a way of life. These concepts are not tied geographically, temporally or even to any specific learning method. The growth and the future of industry is based on the competence of existing personnel. If we have to meet the increasing need for education using existing resources, those resources must be deployed more effectively.

9. THE PRINCIPLES OF OPEN LEARNING

Students have easy access to education. Working adults can best study close to work, with the teacher present either physically or through the medium of communication technology, or via a combination of the two.

There are many sources of education, provided by various centers of excellence. In addition to schools and universities, research institutes, enterprises and specialists in each field can provide education. Schools and universities, however, always **control the quality and level of instruction** and see that education corresponds to the target level of study.

Studies should be linked with present or future tasks, and support one's career. This requires a better combination of academic studies and practice than is being achieved today. Theoretical education in parallel with application training is usually most effective for the student. When "tools" for daily work become insufficient, an actual need to study theory as well becomes most acute.

All teaching and communication methods and means, both traditional and modern, are needed for producing and imparting education. Students can compile their own study programme, e.g. using courses transmitted by satellite such as Euro-PACE programmes, those arranged at the workplace by a university or other educational institute, or study using a PC and written supplementary material. Education can be guided by a teacher authorised by the university or by an expert who can also be from the same company as the students.

For further motivation the possibility to take official examinations should always be included in adult studies. Even though **knowledge is a reward in itself, an examination keeps one studying.** When instruction is produced internationally, the competence acquired through it should be recognised internationally as well.

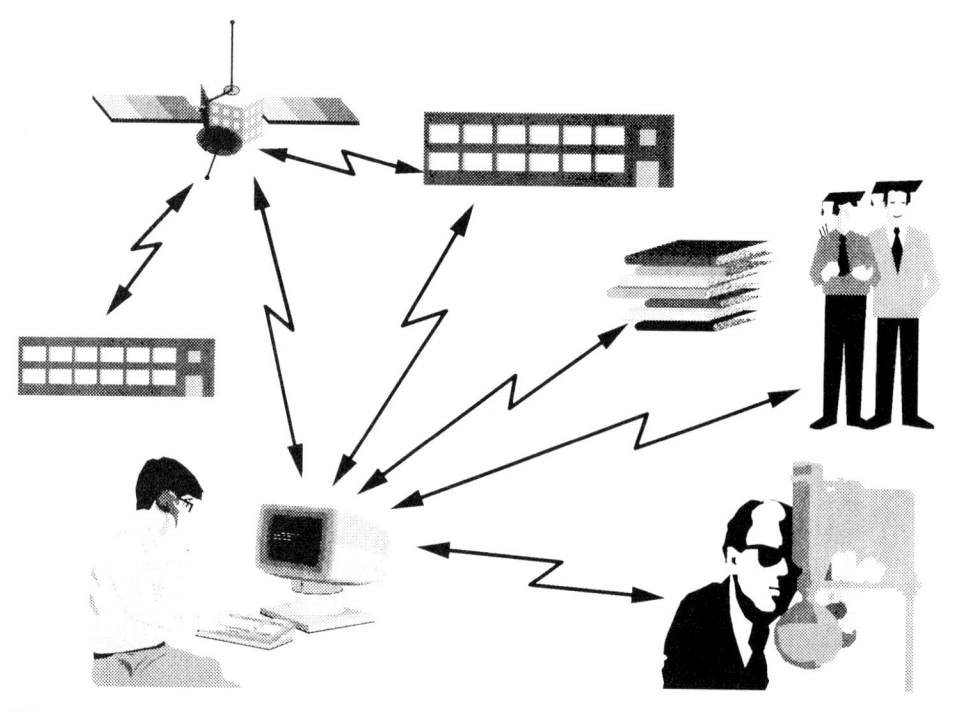

Figure 3. Open learning

10. ORGANISATION BASED ON CO-OPERATION

Adult education calls for flexible co-operation between the education authorities, schools and industry. In an educational sense they form a network in which each has its own area of responsibility and competence.

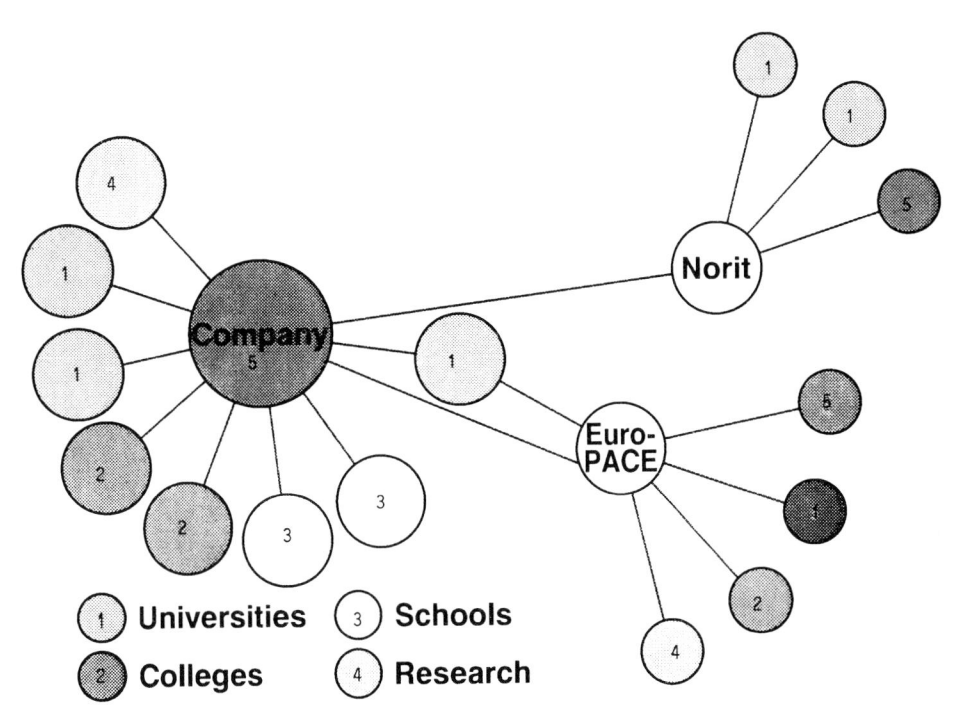

Figure 4. Co-operation in education

Industry selects the subject matter for study and students. **Schools and universities produce the required education and control the level of education in addition to arranging appropriate examinations**, when needed. Schools and universities co-ordinate and select various sources of education to build up a comprehensive study programme. In addition, various **organisations** or wider co-operation between educational institutes are needed in order to bring the various producers of education within the range of mutual channels of communication. Euro-PACE is a typical organisation of this kind, as is the Nordic institute of information technology NORIT.

Upor individual- themselves falls the responsibility to utilise these opportunities for study and to answer for their own professional competence.

11. WORK ON ATTITUDES NEEDED ON ALL LEVELS

The emphasis of education should be shifted quickly from young people to adults. To schools, universities and teachers, adult students are a challenge. Education must meet quite new requirements. Much greater flexibility is needed both in the implementation of educational programmes and in education practice.

Important changes of attitudes are, however, still needed among individuals. Everyone has to take responsibility for their own competitiveness. This shifting of attitudes requires both the means of the media, industry and the contribution of employers and trade unions.

BIBLIOGRAPHY

Barblan, A., and Sadlak, J., (1988), "Higher Education in OECD European Countries: Patterns and Trend in the 1980's", (Internal Memorandum), CRE, Geneva

Beare, H., and Lemke, H., (1987), "The Curriculum and the Economy", OECD, Paris

Boyatzis, R.E., (1982), "The Competent Manager", John Weley, New York

Braddick W.A.J. and McAllister D., (1988) "Management Development Practices in the ERT Group of Companies - A Report and Recommendations", (Internal Memorandum), European Foundation for Management Development, Brussels

Bylander M. and Ros F., (1988), "Final Report of the Higher Education Subcommittee European Round Table", (Internal Memorandum), Västerås and Madrid

Cavallé, C., (1987), "Managing Successfully in a Multicultural Environment. What Does it Mean to Management Development?", European Foundation for Management Development, Brussels

Cerych, L., and Jallade, J.-P., (1984), "Competences and Competition, Training and Education in the Federal Republic of Germany, the United States and Japan", National Economic Development Office and Manpower Services Commission, London

Cerych, L., and Jallade, J.-P., (1986), "The Coming Technological Revolution in Education", A Report to the Dutch Ministry of Education and Science, European Institute of Education and Social Policy, Paris

Cerych, L., and Jallade, J.-P., (1988), "Interactive Video Disks (IVD) in Education, an Assessment Based on Experiments in the U.S. and the U.K.", A report to the Dutch Ministry of Education and Science, European Institute of Education and Social, Paris

Chaplin, A.G.F., (1988), "Vocational Education Across Europe (VET), Report of a Survey of Companies Affiliated to the European Round Table of Industrialists", (Internal Memorandum), Pilkington, St-Helens, U.K.

"Compulsory Schooling in a Changing World", (1983), OECD, Paris

Constable, J., and McCormick, R., (1987), "The Making of British Managers: A Report for the BIM and CBI into Management Training, Education and Development", British Institute of Management, NORTHANTS, United Kingdom

"Demographic Statistics" (1987), Theme 3, Series C, Eurostat, Luxembourg

Easterby-Smith, M., and Tanton, M., (1988), "Strategies and Faculty Development in Business Schools and Management Development Institutions: An International Study", University of Lancaster, United Kingdom

"Effective Engineering Education", (1988), Conference Report, Helsinki University of Technology and Engineering Society, Finland (STS), Melburyhill, SEFI, Helsinki

Eurich, N.P., Hasegawa H., and Sadler Ph., (1986), "Recent Trends in Management Development", European Foundation for Management Development, Brussels

"A European Policy for Europe", (1982), Office for Official Publication of the European Communities, Luxembourg

European Society for Engineering Education, (1986), Joint Europe/North America Continuing Education Forum, Palo Alto (California). Report, SEFI, Brussels

Fonda, N., and Hayes, F.C., (1988), "Education, Training and Economic Performance: Positioning for Turbulent Times", Oxford Review of Economic Policy, Volume IV, Oxford

Grootings, Peter, et al, (1988), "Work and Learning", Presses Interuniversitaires Européennes, Maastricht

Handy, C., (1987), "The Making of Managers: A Report on Management Education, Training and Development in the USA, West Germany, France, Japan and the U.K.", Manpower Services Commission, National Economic Development Office, London, U.K.

Harrison, R., (1987), "Organisation Culture and Quality of Service", AMED, London

Hessler, A., (1988), "Efforts to Change Higher Education Systems in the F.R. Germany and Great Britain", Fundesco, Spain

"Intergovernmental Conference on Education and Economy in a Changing Society", (1987), Issue Papers, OECD, Paris

Jallade, J.-P., (1982), "Alternance Training for Young People: Guidelines for Action", CEDEFOP, Berlin and CEE, Luxembourg

Jallade J.-P., (1988), "Educating Young People for the 21st Century", A report prepared for the Education Committee of the Round Table of European Industrialists", European Institute of Education and Social Policy, Paris

Jallade J.-P., (1988), "La formation professionnelle à l'étranger. Quels enseignements pour la France?", Commissariat Général du Plan, La Documentation Française, Paris

Le Monde, (1988), September 15, 1988, Paris

Lesourne, J., (1988), Education et Société, les défis de l'an 2000", La Découverte, Paris

"Livre Bleu pour une Europe de l'Education et de la Culture", (1987), Ministère de la Culture et de la Communication, Ministère des Affaires Etrangères, Ministère de l'Education Nationale, Ministère Délégué Chargé des Affaires Européennes par la République Française, Paris

Lyman, W., and McKibbin L.E., (1988), "Management Education and Development", McGraw Hill, New York

"Making Europe Work", (1986), A report for the Round Table of European Industrialists, Jernström Offset, Sweden

"Management for the Future", (1988), Ashridge Management College and Foundation for Management Education, United Kingdom

"Meeting of Management Experts on Training of the Adult Labour Force in a Constantly Changing Labour Market", (1988) OECD, Paris

Official Journal of the European Communities, 31 July 1985; 10 December 1987

"Oxford Review on Economic Policy", (Autumn 1988), Oxford University Press, Oxford

Platt, R.R., (1988), "A View of Interactions between Government, Industry and Higher Education in the United Kingdom", Salford University, United Kingdom

"Policies of Transition", (1984), EC Report on the Action Programme, Transition of Young People from Education to Adult and Working Life", IFAPLAN, Brussels

Raffe D. and Tomes N., Center for Educational Sociology, University of Edinburgh

Ros F., (1986), Formacion de técnicos investigadores en tecnologias de la informacion", Fundesco, Madrid

Ros, F., (1987), "Some Comparative Data on Higher Education Systems in Western Europe, North America (North America and Canada) and Japan", Fundesco, Spain

Squires, G., (1987), "Organisation and Content of Studies at the Post-Secondary Level", OECD, Paris

Stoob, F., and Troll, L., (1988), "Das Arbeitsmittelkonzept als Instrumentarium zur Beobachtung des Technologischen Wandels", Institut für Arbeitsmarkt und Berufsförderung Bundesanstalt für Arbeit, Nürnberg

"Structural Adjustment and Economic Performance" (1987), OECD, Paris

"Sweden's Vocational Education in Transition", (1986), Swedish Ministry of Education and Cultural Affairs, Stockholm

UNESCO Statistical Yearbook, (1986), UNESCO, Paris

TERMINOLOGY

Action learning

>A means of intellectual, emotional and physical development through involvement in the solution of real, complex and stressful problems, i.e. learning by doing.

Basic education

>Education necessary to function in society. The compulsory schooling up to 16 years of age and education for the 16-18 age group, whether it is carried out in schools, apprenticeships or in work-based training schemes.

Centre of excellence

>A higher education centre, such as a university, specialising in one or more selected areas of research or academic study.

Certified vocational qualifications

>Qualifications generally recognised by European employers.

CAI

>Computer-assisted instruction.

COMETT

>Community Action Programme in Education and Training for Technology (EC programme).

Compatibility

>Consistency between the levels and contents of vocational or academic degrees awarded in various European countries.

Competence

>The ability to apply knowledge, skills and experience in the solution of problems on a day to day basis.

Core curriculum

>Curriculum leading to a minimum competence for everybody, to which options may be added to suit a person's tastes and activities. Core curriculum elements are present in the curricula of specific subjects.

Courses

>Usually short-term, condensed and limited education programmes with the purpose of giving knowledge in a specific field or subject.

CRE
: Standing Conference of Rectors, Presidents, and Vice-Chancellors of the European Universities, Geneva.

Curriculum
: What is taught and learnt in schools and other educational institutions.

DELTA
: Developing European Learning through Technological Advance (EC programme).

Distance learning (education)
: Open learning referring specifically to learning at a distance from the tutor. Teaching and learning through TV, video programmes, radio or mail.

Dual system of vocational training
: A combination of training programmes in companies and school-based instruction in vocational schools with an average duration of 3 years. Trainees in West Germany, for example, undergo vocational training for 4 days a week in the company and one day at the vocational school. The dual system is used mainly in West Germany, Austria and Switzerland.

Education
: Proficiency in understanding and knowledge within a particular category of skill. An example would be high school, college or university.

Electronic teaching aids
: TV, video, PC's, language laboratories; otherwise known as Computer Aided Learning (CAL) or Interactive Video Disc Learning (IVDL).

ERASMUS
: European Community Action Scheme for the Mobility of University Students (EC programme).

ERT
: European Round Table of Industrialists, Brussels.

European awareness
: A comprehension of and sense of affinity with the cultural and economic values of Europe.

Euro-PACE

    European Programme for Advanced Continuing Education. Euro-PACE is an industry-sponsored and financed distance learning programme based in Paris.

European Economic Space

    EC and EFTA countries.

Fundamental basic skills

    Reading, writing, natural sciences (mathematics, physics, chemistry) and a provision for oral communication in the mother tongue, in English and one other major European language.

Graduate

    A person who has completed studies in an educational institution (college or university) and has been awarded a degree.

Higher education

    Training institutions beyond matriculation, i.e. after finishing secondary level II, like colleges, universities and business schools.

Industrial tutors

    Qualified individuals from industry to help students get the best out of their periods in a company.

Industry inspectors

    Body of individuals from industry responsible for examining current school-based practices in the teaching of a specific set of skills.

In-plant training

    Vocational training in a firm as part of an apprenticeship or within the dual system.

Intermediate university degree

    University degrees below MA level, e.g. BA.

Log book

    Records of a person's personal achievements, illustrating a student's progress in each learning area.

Managerial skills

    Skills related to effective organisation of work and people, and leadership. The planning of human and other resources in an effective way.

Modules

    Self-contained parts of a curriculum.

NORIT

    Nordiskt Institut för Informationsteknik (Nordic programme sponsored and financed by Nordic industries).

Off-the-job training

    Job-related training activities taking place outside normal working hours.

On-the-job training

    Job-related training activities, either as part of a job or closely related to it, taking place during normal working hours.

Open learning

    Any form of teaching, other than by formal course, which enables an individual or individuals to learn at their own pace, at the most convenient time, in optional locations, with minimum support.

Open university

    (See open learning.) In the United Kingdom, not only is there the Open University, there is also the Open Tech for technician training and, more recently, the Open College for people to study at below-degree levels. All of these constitute distance learning approaches with open access to courses.

Partnership

    Training arrangements between schools, universities and other training institutions and individuals.

Post-graduate university degree

    Dr, Ph.D. and Licentiate (Denmark, Finland and Sweden).

Retraining

    Education and training for new skills or updating and upgrading knowledge and skills.

Skill

The ability to carry out a task.

Study programme

A limited field of study, often consisting of several courses or modules.

Tailor-made studies

Studies developed in order to master a specific subject or technology.

TARGET

Joint educational institution and industry project, Thames Valley, UK, financed within the EC COMETT programme.

Targetted studies

Limited studies in a specific field with the purpose of giving comprehension and mastery of that field.

Training

Providing the understanding and knowledge along with the skill or ability to do the job. A good example would be on-the-job training combining classroom and "hands on" lessons.

Transferability

Recognition of vocational or academic degrees in European countries other than those in which they are awarded.

Trilingualism

Mastering one's mother tongue, English and one other major European languages.

VET

Vocational education and training.

MAIN CONTRIBUTORS

Mr. Bill BRADDICK is Director General of the European Foundation for Management Development, Brussels. He has been Deputy Principal of Ashridge Management College, UK, and is a Board member of the International Schools of Business Management and the European Institute for Advanced Studies in Management.

Mr. Magnus BYLANDER is Manager of Human Resources Development with Asea Brown Boveri. He has a master's degree in engineering from the Royal Institute of Technology, Stockholm.

Mr. Tony CHAPLIN is Head of Group Training and Development with Pilkington plc, UK. He has a degree in mechanical engineering and is a member of several prestigious UK organisations in education and training.

Mr. Chris HAYES is Chairman of the Prospect Centre, a UK consulting organisation. Originally a lecturer in mathematical physics, he later became a Deputy Chief Executive in the Manpower Services Commission.

Dr. Jean-Pierre JALLADE is Deputy Director of the European Institute of Education and Social Policy and a regular consultant to the EC in Brussels. He has written extensively on education and unemployment.

Mrs. Leenamaija JARENKO is Vice President, Education and Training, of the Nokia Group and Director of Nokia Training Center. She is responsible for the wide development and training programmes of Nokia personnel and has written extensively on education and information.

Dr. Kari KAIRAMO is Chairman and CEO of Nokia, Finland and a member of the ERT, whose Standing Working Group on Education he chairs. He has held various industrial posts in Finland and the Americas. In addition to sitting on the boards of major Finnish and European companies, he is also engaged in the top leadership of many industrial and educational organisations throughout Europe, in addition to holding numerous honourary offices.

Dr. Kerstin KEEN is Managing Director of Volvo Competence Development Corporation in Gothenburg. She has been a member of the Swedish Parliament and has both secondary school and university teaching experience.

Mr. Horst LEMKE is a consultant on vocational training to the OECD, the EC Commission and national institutions. He is an adviser to industrial training authorities in several countries and has been a head of department at the Federal Ministry of Education and Science in West Germany.

Mr. Desmond McALLISTER is a partner of The Development Consulting Group, Brussels. He was formerly a Director of ITT Europe, and has worked as a consultant with the Grubb Institute of Behavioural Studies, UK, and the Giovanni Agnelli Foundation, Italy.

Professor Dr. Matti OTALA is Senior Vice President and Chief Technical Officer of the Nokia group. He has been professor of electronics in several universities in different countries and worked as Chief Engineer in various industrial companies in the U.S.A., Japan and Europe.

Dr. Jan-Peter PAUL is Secretary General of the ERT Standing Education Working Group. He was has been the Head of Economic Information with Nokia, Finland and has been Finland's Trade Commissioner in Pretoria and New York. He has published several scientific books and papers on economic and social subjects.

Dr. Fransisco ROS is Director of Industrial Promotion and Development with Telefónica de Espana S.A., Spain. He holds Ph.D. degrees from the University of Madrid and MIT.

Mr. Giovanni TESTA is Director of the ISVOR FIAT Management Centre, with responsibility for managerial training of top FIAT management. He has a law degree.